PRAISE FOR THE NEW TEAM HABITS

Leadership has one responsibility: to grow your people. The three habits are steps to set those conditions. It's really a simple equation . . . grow the people, the people grow the organization, and the organization grows the results.

Howard Behar
former President of Starbucks

This short, visual, and practical book will make you smile, think, work, and practice so you and your team get better and more responsive.

Tom Vander Ark
CEO of Getting Smart

The traditional education system was set up as a single-player sport. You were responsible for your work, your assignments, your test scores, your grades, your behavior, and so on. If you work in education, this model continued throughout your career as an educator.

The problem is we now live in a team-based world, and unless you played a team sport, most of us never learned how to be part of a creative and productive team. We never learned the habits and skills critical to team effectiveness. We certainly didn't have a guide or the ability to practice good habits.

This guide is a playbook, specifically focused on helping teams build habits as a collective unit, instead of as individuals. This step-by-step guide allows teams to practice battle-tested activities that will help them develop productive and practical habits of learning, meetings, and projects.

Any team that works through this playbook will come out as a more effective and productive team on the other side!

Jaime Casap
Google Education Evangelist

Shared habits are at the root of culture, which makes **The NEW Team Habits** an excellent guide for building a strong team culture that delivers for our students. Far too few thought leaders pay enough attention to these operational questions. Bravo to Anthony Kim, Keara Mascareñaz, Kawai Lai, and Education Elements for digging in here.

Michael Horn
co-author of **Choosing College** and
Head of Strategy of The Entangled Group

Equity, diversity, and inclusion are a high priority for many districts across the country. A genuine commitment and a strong understanding of how to secure the presence of these tenets in the teaching and learning landscape will continue to be at the center stage of visionary and innovative strategic plans. **The NEW Team Habits** has the potential to provide actionable approaches to making equity, diversity, and inclusion part of our daily practice.

Jose Dotres
Chief Human Capital Officer of
Miami-Dade County Public Schools

The *new* Team Habits

DEDICATION

To my precious wife, Angela, who continues to give me space to devote to my passions. If it wasn't for her gifts to give me time to explore and learn, I wouldn't have been able to write this third book. My mother, Kay, who somehow seeded me with grit and discipline to achieve goals I set. I live life to learn, transfer knowledge, and to evolve. Everyone around me who contributes to that, I'm forever grateful. —**Anthony**

For everyone who teaches, listens, and fights for what's right. For my loving, generous, joyful family and friends. And for L, my great love and true partner in life. —**Keara**

To the educators who are challenging the status quo in our education system. I hope the ideas of this book begin to change the culture of the system and create environments where educators and students can thrive. —**Kawai**

The *new* Team Habits

A Guide to the New School Rules

Anthony Kim | Keara Mascareñaz | Kawai Lai

CORWIN

For information:

Corwin
A SAGE Company
2455 Teller Road
Thousand Oaks, California 91320
(800) 233–9936
www.corwin.com

SAGE Publications Ltd.
1 Oliver's Yard
55 City Road
London, EC1Y 1SP
United Kingdom

SAGE Publications India Pvt. Ltd.
B 1/I 1 Mohan Cooperative Industrial Area
Mathura Road, New Delhi 110 044
India

SAGE Publications Asia-Pacific Pte. Ltd.
18 Cross Street #10–10/11/12
China Square Central
Singapore 048423

Publisher: Arnis Burvikovs
Development Editor: Desirée A. Bartlett
Senior Editorial Assistant: Eliza Erickson
Production Editor: Tori Mirsadjadi
Copy Editor: Amy Marks
Typesetter: Integra
Proofreader: Liann Lech
Cover Designer: Gail Buschman
Marketing Manager: Sharon Pendergast

Copyright © 2020 by Anthony Kim, Keara Mascareñaz, and Kawai Lai

Library of Congress Cataloging-in-Publication Data

Names: Kim, Anthony, author. | Mascarenaz, Keara, author. | Lai, Kawai, author.

Title: The NEW team habits : a guide to the new school rules / Anthony Kim, Keara Mascarenaz, Kawai Lai.

Description: Thousand Oaks, California : Corwin, [2020] | Includes bibliographical references.

Identifiers: LCCN 2019023350 | ISBN 9781544375038 (spiral bound) | ISBN 9781544375014 (epub) | ISBN 9781544375007 (epub) | ISBN 9781544375021 (adobe pdf)

Subjects: LCSH: School management and organization. | Educational leadership.

Classification: LCC LB2805 .K478 2020 | DDC 371.2–dc23 LC record available at https://lccn.loc.gov/2019023350

Printed in the United States of America.

This book is printed on acid-free paper.

MIX
Paper from
responsible sources
FSC® C005010

19 20 21 22 23 10 9 8 7 6 5 4 3 2 1

Contents

ACKNOWLEDGMENTS

Many people inspired us to develop the ideas in this guide and encouraged us to share them with other organizations that are looking to evolve how their teams work together. The educators we work with, our families and friends, our professional networks, and our work colleagues all informed what we present to you here.

Every day we work with educators across the country, learning from them, experimenting together, and refining what works. We especially want to recognize a few organizations that gave us the opportunity to validate some of these practices while they were still in development: Richard DelMoro and Amy Creeden at Enlarged City School District of Middletown, Jose Dotres at Miami-Dade County Public Schools, Rob Anderson at Boulder Valley School District, and Jenn Beagan at Allegheny Intermediate Unit 3. We've also learned so much from organizations outside of education, including Alexis Gonzales-Black, coauthor of **The NEW School Rules: 6 Vital Practices for Thriving and Responsive Schools**, and the teams at Responsive Conference, The Culture Conference, Play on Purpose, August, The Ready, Parabol, Responsive Org, and VizLit.

We are honored that **The NEW School Rules** was so successful and became a bestseller for Corwin, and that our publisher prompted us to develop a guide that goes deeper and focuses on even more actionable concepts. The early adopters of **The NEW School Rules** provided us valuable insight into how to approach this guide, so we thank the hundreds of teams that started book studies, shared ideas with us, and became ambassadors for these responsive practices in their own teams and districts. These early adopters include the school board at Juab School District, the Pennsylvania Association of School Administrators, Daniel Woestman and David Carson at Belvidere School District 100, and Jill Ries at Racine Unified School District.

Finally, this guide would not have been possible without the incredible team at Education Elements helping us to test and refine these practices internally and with our district partners—particularly Gabrielle Hewitt, who brought responsive practices to life with stories, activities, and workshops; Andrea Goetchius, who led the way with the development of The SEPAD Method and our approach to leadership development; and Megan Campion, who honed our one-on-one responsive coaching practice.

Why We Wrote This Guide

We created this step-by-step guide because we found that although leaders often understand why new practices matter, they struggle to build buy-in, transfer knowledge to others, and make changes that are the right size—big enough to make an impact, but not so big as to overwhelm themselves or their teams. This guide is specifically focused on teams and helping them build habits as a unit, instead of as individuals. The activities have been battle-tested as we facilitated learning and coaching for hundreds of leadership teams across the country.

This guide provides a light introduction to the six new school rules. If you want to develop a deeper understanding of the rules and their philosophical grounding, we recommend revisiting the book or our website:

www.newschoolrules.com

Why Does This Guide Focus on One Team?

This guide focuses on teams as the unit of change. For a habit to take root, it needs to be learned, practiced, and used by an entire team. **The NEW Team Habits** specifically supports you to make changes within one team. Once you've engaged one team in shifting their habits, it is easier to build and customize these habits with other teams and eventually across the organization.

YOUR STEP-BY-STEP GUIDE

You may wonder why we aren't helping you create organization-wide change from the start. After all, if you are reading this guide you are likely an organizational leader. Too often we see leaders try to make shifts at the organizational level before meaningful work has been done with individuals to shift mindsets and build skills, or with teams to develop trust and create shared understanding, relying on a few "hero" leaders to drive the change. But, to last, change needs to be driven and supported by the entire team. Therefore, this guide will focus on individual- and team-level changes first. In doing so, we will establish team habits that build a foundation for lasting changes that you can spread across your organization and sustain in the future.

CHAPTER 1
Why Team Habits Matter

Why Responsive Orgs Matter

You likely have some interest in changing the way work happens in your organization. You are part of a group of leaders working across sectors who are seeking to improve the way their organizations function. These leaders are part of a movement to create more responsive organizations.

The responsive org movement has gained momentum as leaders have sought new ways to design and run their teams and organizations at large. The folks at responsive.org have defined this kind of organizational design:

"Responsive organizations are built to learn and respond rapidly through the open flow of information; encouraging experimentation and learning on rapid cycles; and organizing as a network of employees, customers, and partners motivated by shared purpose."

As our world has become more digital, connected, and complex, there is a need to shift to a more responsive organizational design that values the diverse needs of humans inside of the organization and the rapid changes in the world outside of the organization. We see organizational design as a constant evolution. Our foundational designs shift as the nature of work, the distribution of power, and the needs of the people change.

" When trust is extended, it breeds responsibility in return. Emulation and peer pressure regulates the system better than hierarchy ever could. "

—Frederic Laloux

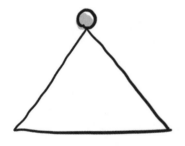

monarchical

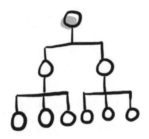

hierarchical

functional

responsive

EVOLUTION OF ORGANIZATIONAL DESIGN

The Rules of Responsive Organizations

Since Anthony Kim and Alexis Gonzales-Black published **The NEW School Rules: 6 Vital Practices for Thriving and Responsive Schools,** we have had the opportunity to use the six new school rules with hundreds of education leaders who are seeking to improve the way their teams collaborate, make decisions, and work together.

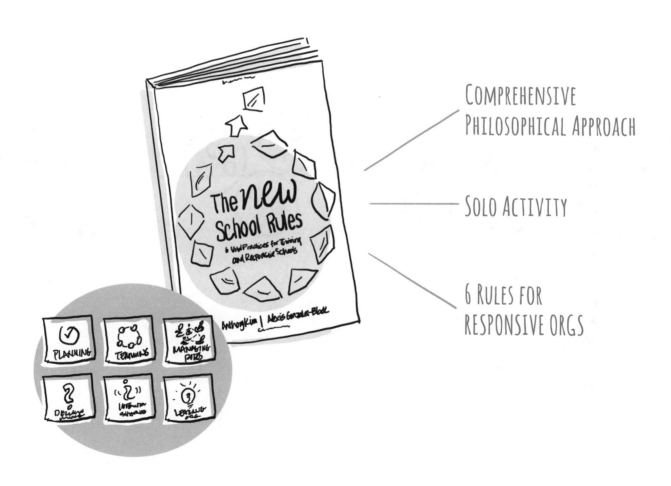

Comprehensive
Philosophical Approach

Solo Activity

6 Rules for
Responsive Orgs

How to Turn Rules Into Habits

When implementing a new set of ideas and practices like the new school rules, there are three routes you might take. Implementing the rules on your own is easy and inexpensive. However, this approach can be time consuming and overwhelming and requires incredible self-discipline. Hiring a coach to guide your implementation provides effective and customized support, but can be expensive. Using a step-by-step guide like **The NEW Team Habits** provides some of the support of a coach with the flexibility and cost efficiency that come from implementing on your own.

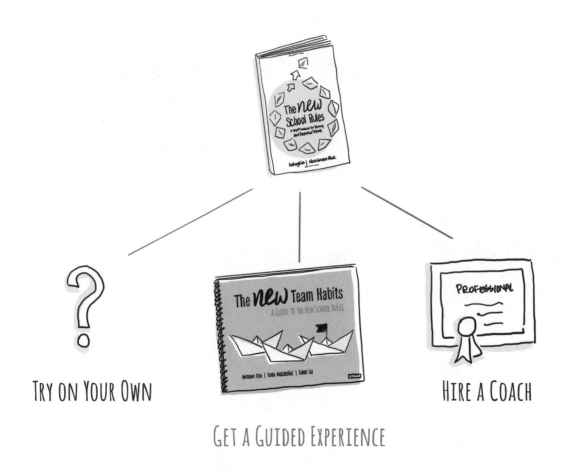

TRY ON YOUR OWN

GET A GUIDED EXPERIENCE

HIRE A COACH

How We Think About Change

Change occurs at three levels: individual, team, and organizational. We see leaders often focused on individual- or organizational-level change, and this guide is meant to shift the focus to team-level change. We see teams as a critical unit for making lasting change across an organization.

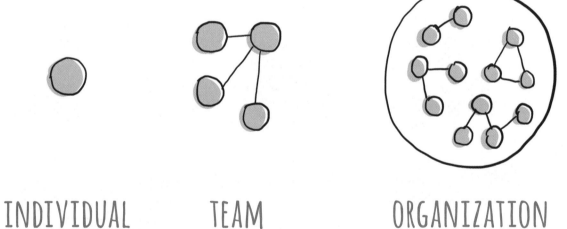

INDIVIDUAL   TEAM   ORGANIZATION

The Habits of Responsive Teams

The NEW School Rules offers a philosophical approach as well as concrete practice and experiments for each of the six rules. Yet we've found that leaders have needed even more explicit guidance to help their teams build knowledge and apply the rules. These habits bring together the new school rules in a way that makes them easier to apply in everyday work. This guide focuses on teams as the unit to drive change across an organization. It provides a step-by-step guide to build new team habits for learning, meetings, and projects. Although there are more habits you can build in these three areas, we focus on one habit for each, specifically to get your team started in shifting the way work happens.

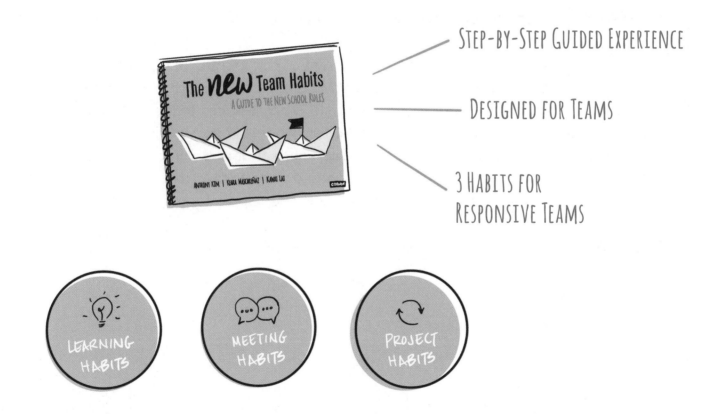

The NEW Team Habits
A GUIDE TO THE NEW SCHOOL RULES

ANTHONY KIM | KEARA MASCAREÑAZ | KAWAI LAI

Step-by-Step Guided Experience

Designed for Teams

3 Habits for Responsive Teams

LEARNING HABITS

MEETING HABITS

PROJECT HABITS

What Is a Habit?

A habit is a regular tendency, behavior, or practice. Habits are the things we do so often they become second nature.

Some smart people have written about how to build habits, including Charles Duhigg, Elena Aguilar, Jeremy Dean, and James Clear. Duhigg articulates the process of building a habit as cue, routine, reward; Clear as cue, craving, response, reward. In both cases the focus for their work is the individual and how a single person can build a new habit for health, home, work, or love.

Just as personal habits impact the development of our identity (e.g., if I run every day, I am a runner; if I smoke every day, I am a smoker), our work habits impact the development of our leadership style. Many leaders focus on trying to change their individual leadership habits. This work is important, but we have found that individual leaders often build habits that end with them or falter without the support of their team. We see a need to help teams build habits in order to shift the way work happens and develop a team identity.

To learn more about habits, visit www.newteamhabits.com/habits.

Just like individual habits, team habits require practice and discipline. Team habits are important because they

1. Create consistent practice across the group for quicker learning and sharing
2. Involve everyone in the change rather than relying on a single person to shoulder the success or failure of a practice
3. Support habits to spread more quickly as members of a single team amplify their habits with other teams they are a part of

Team habits should be consistent across a single team but do not need to be identical across the organization. Each team has its own pulse and shape, and its habits should reflect this.

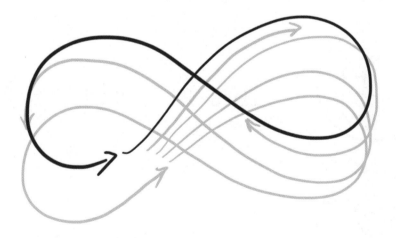

HABITS BECOME SECOND NATURE

Small Habits Connect to a Larger Purpose

In this guide, we have articulated three small habits that can help your team achieve better learning, meetings, and projects.

 **Learning: We talk about mistakes**

 **Meeting: We lead check-ins**

 **Project: We kick off work**

A small habit can have a tiny ripple effect, which can then lead to a greater purpose or big ripple effect. For each of the small habits below, there is a larger purpose.

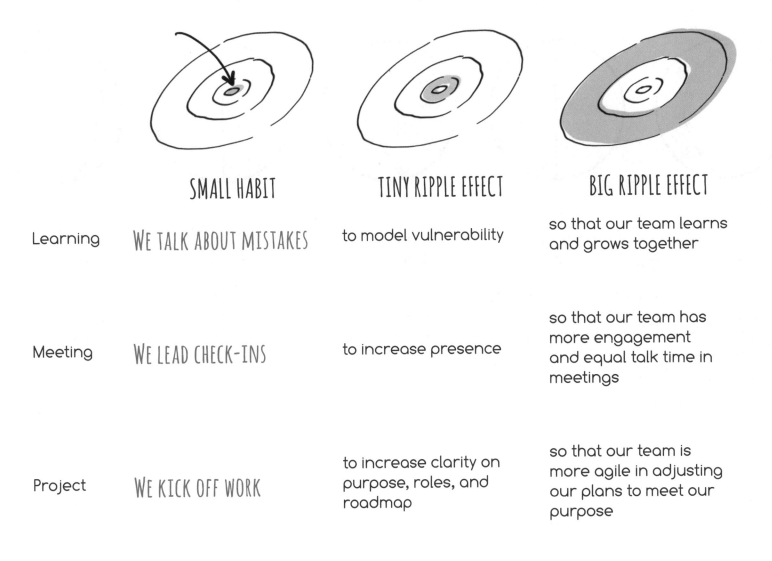

	SMALL HABIT	TINY RIPPLE EFFECT	BIG RIPPLE EFFECT
Learning	WE TALK ABOUT MISTAKES	to model vulnerability	so that our team learns and grows together
Meeting	WE LEAD CHECK-INS	to increase presence	so that our team has more engagement and equal talk time in meetings
Project	WE KICK OFF WORK	to increase clarity on purpose, roles, and roadmap	so that our team is more agile in adjusting our plans to meet our purpose

The SEPAD Method: 5 Steps to Build Team Habits

 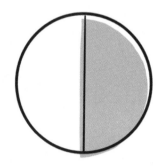  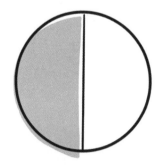 

SPARK	EXPAND	PRACTICE	APPLY	DEBRIEF
Inspiration to illustrate why the habit needs to change	Resource or tool to build understanding of the habit	Activity to practice the habit in a safe environment	Plan for trying the habit in the real world	Reflection on trying the habit + future iterations

As we work with leadership teams to develop responsive habits, we use the five steps of The SEPAD Method. Each chapter is oriented around these five steps and includes resources, activities, and a time estimate for the step.

SPARK — 5–15 minutes

It is essential to spark inspiration and curiosity about why a concept matters before launching into knowledge building. Starting with the why is a step that is often skipped and one that we see as critical to building buy-in and alignment.

EXPAND — 30–45 minutes

Teams need time for explicit knowledge and skill building when introducing new ways of working. The time to expand not only grows every team member's knowledge base, but it also helps to provide opportunities to build connection, collaboration, and trust across the team.

PRACTICE — 15–25 minutes

All successful teams practice skills before applying them in the real world. Practice is a critical part for any shift and provides opportunities to try using new habits in small, safe ways before bringing them back to the real world.

APPLY — 10–15 minutes

After practicing in a safe environment, we provide time to plan how to take each habit back to the real world, with specific guidance around how to determine a goal, hypothesis, and supporting actions to clarify what we're doing, how we're doing it, and what we expect the outcome to be.

DEBRIEF — 15–30 minutes

Structured debrief activities provide time to reflect on how our real-world habit application went. This is a time to share successes and learning across the team. This reflection drives iterations and accelerates learning.

Putting SEPAD Into a Training Plan

We recommend taking one month to learn each habit and complete all five steps of The SEPAD Method for that habit. This should start with a 90-minute team session to SPARK inspiration, EXPAND your knowledge, PRACTICE the habit, and make a plan to APPLY the habit in real life. Following this session, set aside three weeks for applying the habit on your own. Finally, come back together as a group for a 30-minute DEBRIEF on what worked, what didn't, and what you want to try next.

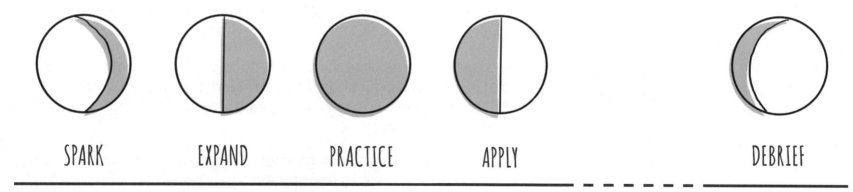

| SPARK | EXPAND | PRACTICE | APPLY | | DEBRIEF |

TEAM SESSION		TRY THE HABIT	TEAM SESSION
90 minutes to Spark, Expand, Practice, and Apply		3 weeks	30 minutes to Debrief

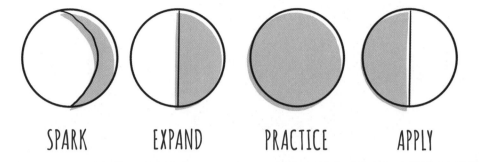

	SPARK	EXPAND	PRACTICE	APPLY		DEBRIEF
LEARNING HABIT: We Talk About Mistakes	Mr. Whiskers 15 min	Psychological Safety 35 min	Triad Share 25 min	Plan to Talk About Mistakes 10 min	Try the Habit 3 weeks	Reflect and Share 30 min
DURATION: 1 MONTH						
MEETING HABIT: We Lead Check-Ins	Top 10 Race 15 min	How Google Builds the Perfect Team 20 min	Try a Check-In 40 min	Plan to Use a Check-In 10 min	Try the Habit 3 weeks	Partner Reflection 30 min
DURATION: 1 MONTH						
PROJECT HABIT: We Kick Off Work	The Great Kick-Off 15 min	Why Kick-Offs Matter 20 min	Role Play Kick-Off 35 min	Plan to Kick Off Work 15 min	Try the Habit 3 weeks	Quadrant Reflection 30 min
DURATION: 1 MONTH						

Why Teams Are Using This Guide

> " Our team is going through a time of transition.
> We've lost and added a number of team members and
> need to learn how to work together. "

—Superintendent in Mid West district

> " Our district cabinet meetings are tough. They last three
> hours or more and leave everyone feeling burnt out and
> overwhelmed. Only one or two people actively participate.
> Everyone else thinks they're a waste of time. "

—District leader in East Coast district

> " Many of our team members are veterans, who have
> been here a long time and have set patterns for doing
> things. Our team simply isn't a learning team. We do
> things the way they have always been done. "

—Principal in West Coast district

CHAPTER 2

Getting Started

How Do We Begin?

The first chapter introduced this book as a step-by-step guide for one team to shift their habits to be more responsive. We recommend following the chapters and activities in order to make sure you are effectively building buy-in, creating inspiration, expanding knowledge, providing opportunities to practice and test habits, and reflecting and adjusting. This chapter details the steps and activities to prepare your team for this work together and primes your team for the Learning Habit: We Talk About Mistakes. The activities in this chapter should take about 90 minutes to complete, including 30 minutes of independent planning for you as the team lead and a 60-minute, in-person session with your team.

1, 2, 3 to Get Started . . . .

We recommend that you, as the sponsor of this work, take these three actions to get started with selecting, communicating with, and kicking off with your team.

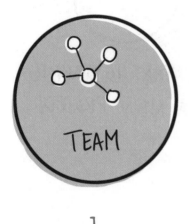

1

Select one small team (ideally fewer than 10 people)

2

Communicate with this team why you're doing this work

3

Bring the team together to launch your work

(this first gathering should be for 60 minutes)

Which Team Should I Choose?

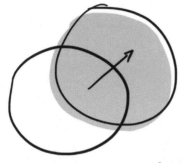

TEAM THAT IS IN TRANSITION

TEAM THAT IS TAKING ON A NEW PROJECT

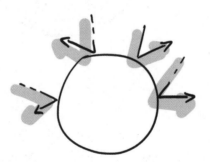

TEAM THAT IS NOT WORKING EFFECTIVELY

First, Select Your Team

For your first time through this guide, we recommend you start with one small team (ideally fewer than 10 people).

WHICH TEAM AM I WORKING WITH? WHY?

LIST TEAM MEMBERS HERE

-
-
-
-
-

-
-
-
-
-

Next, Bring Your Team Together

We recommend you send a quick note to your team letting them know why you're bringing them together for this work. Modify our sample e-mail on the next page by incorporating the why you articulated on the preceding page. You can find e-mail samples and additional resources at www.newteamhabits.com/habits.

Sample E-Mail To Team

WHY?

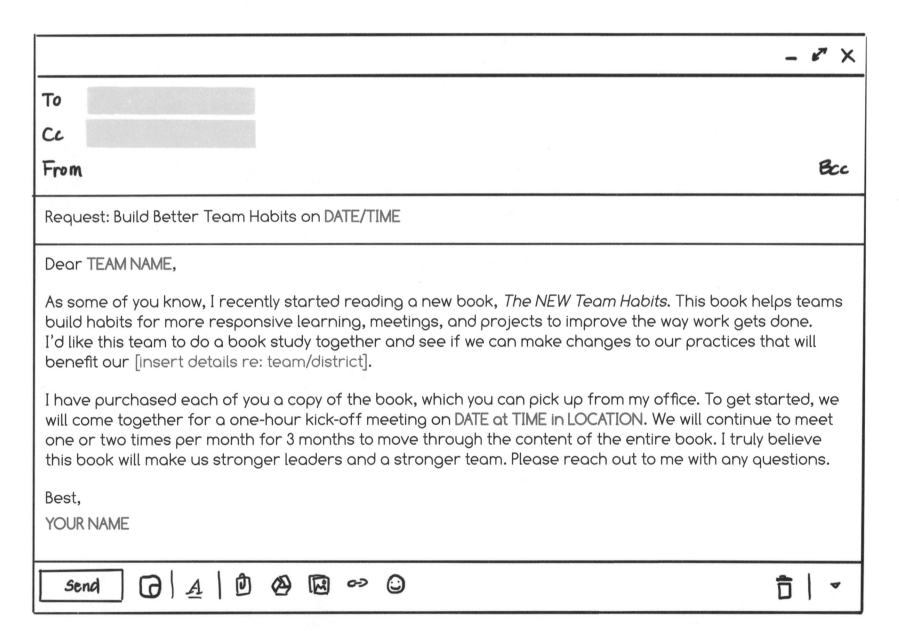

To

Cc

From   Bcc

Request: Build Better Team Habits on DATE/TIME

Dear TEAM NAME,

As some of you know, I recently started reading a new book, *The NEW Team Habits*. This book helps teams build habits for more responsive learning, meetings, and projects to improve the way work gets done. I'd like this team to do a book study together and see if we can make changes to our practices that will benefit our [insert details re: team/district].

I have purchased each of you a copy of the book, which you can pick up from my office. To get started, we will come together for a one-hour kick-off meeting on DATE at TIME in LOCATION. We will continue to meet one or two times per month for 3 months to move through the content of the entire book. I truly believe this book will make us stronger leaders and a stronger team. Please reach out to me with any questions.

Best,
YOUR NAME

Send

⊙ ONCE THE TEAM IS TOGETHER . . .

LAUNCH

As a team, take about 60 minutes in person to move through these six activities together. This will prime your team to get started with this work and prepare you to launch learning about the first habit. We recommend that one member of your team serves as timekeeper to ensure you get through all six actions in the next hour.

1. Complete CIA Challenge (10 min)
2. Reflect on Tom Northrup quote (2 min)
3. Read Chapter 1 of this book (10 min)
4. Create a team why statement (10 min)
5. Create a team learning plan (10 min)
6. Define team commitments to this work (10 min)

The CIA Challenge: Steps 1-3

 10 Minutes  Interact as a Team

This activity should take 10 minutes to complete. We recommend playing an upbeat song during step 2 to amp up the energy and having someone take notes during steps 4 and 5. Steps 1-3 should take about 5 minutes.

1. Break into teams of two or three people.
2. In your teams, detail five ways you could sabotage an enemy organization from the inside. Rules of the game:
   a. The goal is to remain in the organization and prevent it from achieving its goals.
   b. No violence is allowed.
   c. The first team to identify five strategies wins!

3. Have each team briefly share one or two of their favorite sabotage strategies. No need to take notes. This is just to share ideas.

Five Ways to Sabotage an Enemy Org From the Inside				

The CIA Challenge: Steps 4–5

The challenge you just completed is based on actual missions CIA operatives have undertaken. The image below is from a 1940s CIA manual. Take 5 minutes to discuss the following two questions as a group to close out this challenge (you can use the next page to take notes on your discussion).

4. Revisit your list on the previous page. Have you experienced any of the strategies that your groups brainstormed in your current organization?

5. Teams and organizations often are designed for self-sabotage, with too many processes, unclear decision making, and habits that undermine buy-in. What does this challenge have you thinking about regarding why we need to build new team habits for working?

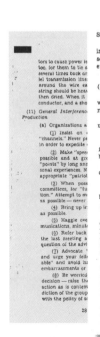

Take Notes During Group Conversation

Have you experienced any of these sabotage strategies in your current team or organization?

What does this challenge have you thinking about regarding why we need to build new team habits for work?

> " All organizations are perfectly designed to get the results they are now getting. If we want different results, we must change the way we do things. "
>
> —Tom Northrup, author of
> *5 Hidden Mistakes CEOs Make*

What Does This Quote Make Me Think About?

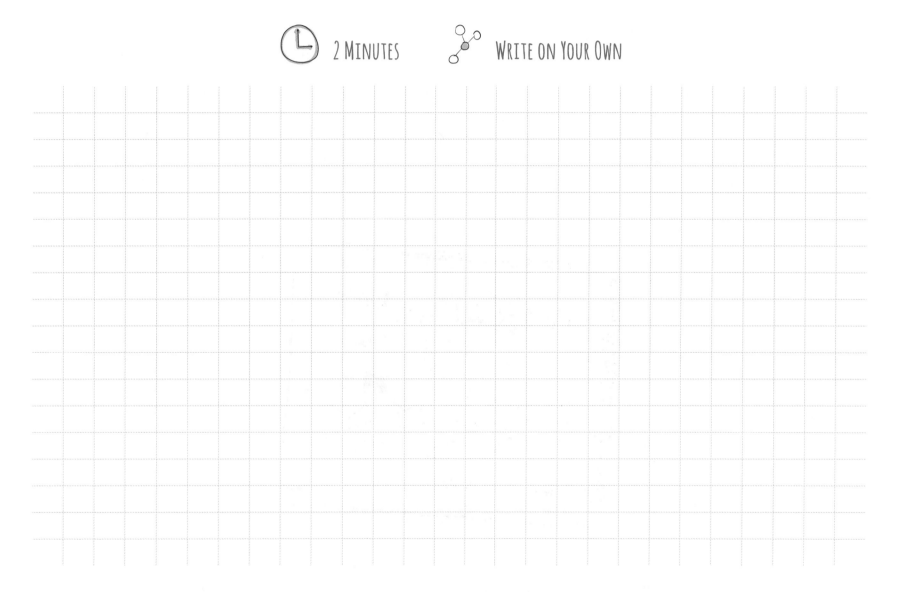

🕐 2 Minutes   ⚛ Write on Your Own

Read Chapter 1: Why Team Habits Matter

 10 Minutes    Read on Your Own

To ensure your team is aligned on the framing and purpose of this guide, take 10 minutes as a team now to read Chapter 1, "Why Team Habits Matter." This context will set up your team to complete the final activities for getting started, which are outlined in this chapter, including creating a why statement, creating a learning plan, and aligning on commitments.

Capture Notes + Ideas From the Reading

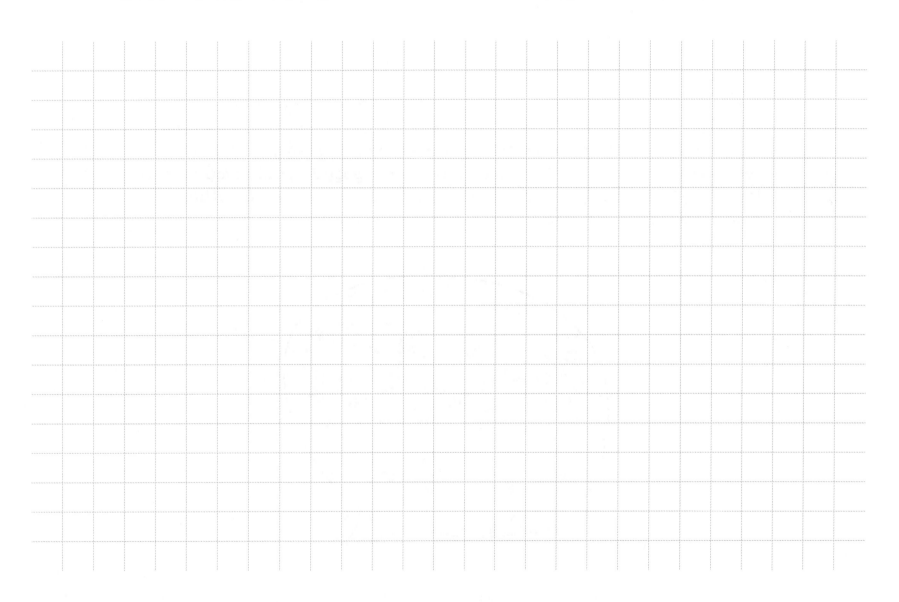

Discuss Why This Matters for Our Team

 10 Minutes    Interact as a Team

Discuss as a group: Why do responsive team habits matter for your team and your organization more broadly? Your team leader shared some thoughts in his or her initial e-mail to this team. You might use inspiration from the CIA Challenge, your personal reflection to Tom Northrup's quote on page 30, or what you learned in reading Chapter 1. At the end of your 5-minute discussion, the goal will be to capture your team's why in one sentence on the next page.

Record Our Team's Why

In one or two sentences, record why building responsive team habits matters for this team and your organization more broadly. The goal is to align as an entire team on one statement that you can return to throughout this work.

CREATE OUR LEARNING PLAN

 10 MINUTES    INTERACT AS A TEAM

To build the team habits to make your learning, meetings, and projects more responsive, we recommend dedicating 3 months to completing all of the activities in the book, meeting two times per month. We have included a recommended learning plan on the next page. Take 10 minutes to fill in the specific dates and times you will meet as a team on that page. You can get a printable poster on our website at **www.newteamhabits .com/habits**. You might start with just the dates for the first habit on learning (1 month), or you might fill in all dates for learning, meeting, and project habits (3 months). Many teams we work with love to color in each step as they complete it.

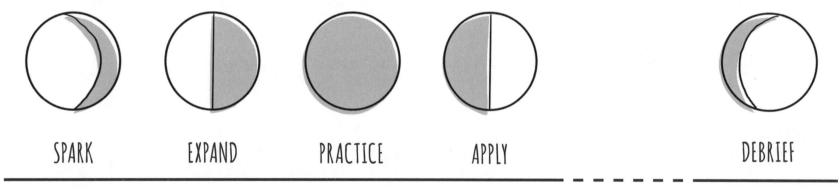

SPARK	EXPAND	PRACTICE	APPLY		DEBRIEF
	TEAM SESSION			TRY THE HABIT	TEAM SESSION
	90 minutes to Spark, Expand, Practice, and Apply			3 weeks	30 minutes to Debrief

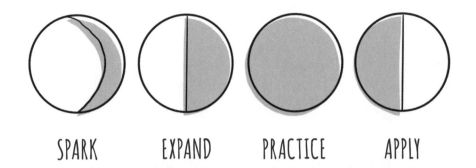

	SPARK	EXPAND	PRACTICE	APPLY		DEBRIEF

LEARNING HABIT:
We Talk About Mistakes

DURATION:
1 Month

	Mr. Whiskers 15 min	Psychological Safety 35 min	Triad Share 25 min	Plan to Talk About Mistakes 10 min	Try the Habit 3 weeks	Reflect and Share 30 min

90-MIN SESSION DATE/TIME: _____   30-MIN DEBRIEF DATE/TIME: _____

MEETING HABIT:
We Lead Check-Ins

DURATION:
1 Month

	Top 10 Race 15 min	How Google Builds the Perfect Team 20 min	Try a Check-In 40 min	Plan to Use a Check-In 10 min	Try the Habit 3 weeks	Partner Reflection 30 min

90-MIN SESSION DATE/TIME: _____   30-MIN DEBRIEF DATE/TIME: _____

PROJECT HABIT:
We Kick Off Work

DURATION:
1 Month

	The Great Kick-Off 15 min	Why Kick-Offs Matter 20 min	Role Play Kick-Off 35 min	Plan to Kick Off Work 15 min	Try the Habit 3 weeks	Quadrant Reflection 30 min

90-MIN SESSION DATE/TIME: _____   30-MIN DEBRIEF DATE/TIME: _____

Define Team Commitments

 10 Minutes    Discuss as a Team

Now that you have an inspiration for why this work matters, a clear why statement, and a learning plan with specific dates and times, take a few final minutes to make commitments to each other and to this work. We've included some sample commitments below. Talk as a group, and record any team commitments on the next page.

SAMPLE TEAM COMMITMENTS

- We commit to attending every team session for the next 3 months.

- We commit to starting and ending our sessions on time.

- We commit to trying habits in our real work in between our team sessions.

OUR TEAM COMMITMENTS

CHAPTER 3

Learning Habit:
We Talk About Mistakes

The NEW School Power Rules for Learning Habits

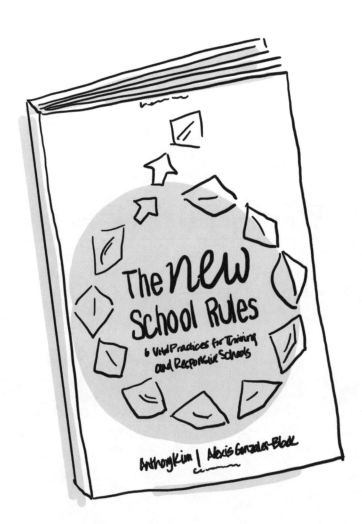

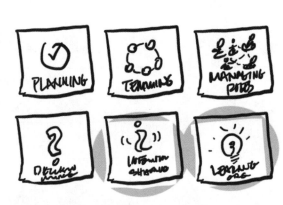

To effectively shift your team learning habits to be more responsive, you will need an understanding of the key principles from these two new school rules. If you want additional context, we recommend revisiting the original chapters in the book or visiting www.newschoolrules.com.

RULE #5 SHARING INFO

Harness the Flow and Let Information Go

Your team's learning culture is only as strong as your team's sharing culture.

- Commit to true transparency by defaulting to open instead of closed systems for sharing information.
- Think about the expiration date of information to make sure you're sharing the right level of detail at the right cadence.

RULE #6 LEARNING ORG

Schools Grow When People Grow

Your team can learn and adapt when you support individuals on the team to learn and adapt.

- Look beyond "best practices" to promote active problem solving and innovation.
- Think of yourself as an agent of change, as opposed to a subject of change.

Where Are We in the Training Plan?

We are in the first of three habit-building cycles. As a team, you're aligned on your why and your timeline for building habits. This first cycle focuses on building the Learning Habit: We Talk About Mistakes.

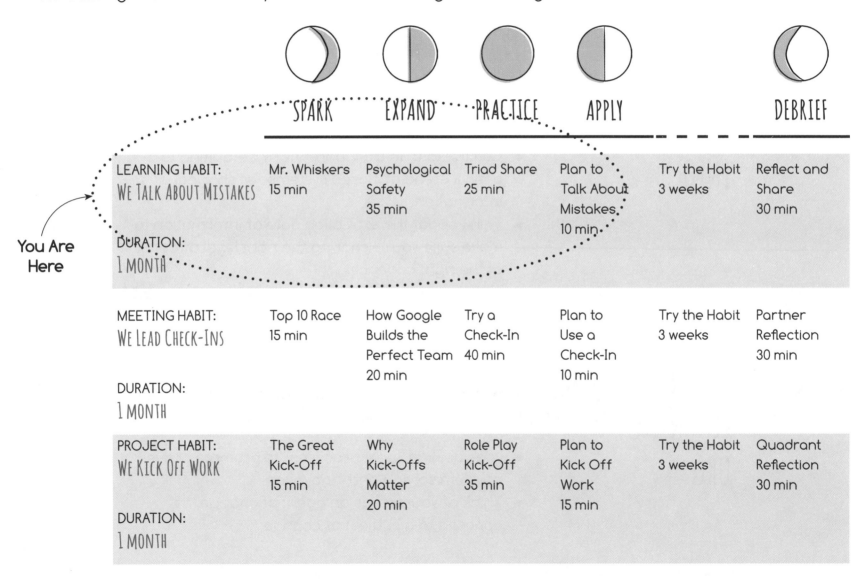

	SPARK	EXPAND	PRACTICE	APPLY		DEBRIEF
LEARNING HABIT: We Talk About Mistakes	Mr. Whiskers 15 min	Psychological Safety 35 min	Triad Share 25 min	Plan to Talk About Mistakes 10 min	Try the Habit 3 weeks	Reflect and Share 30 min
DURATION: 1 MONTH						
MEETING HABIT: We Lead Check-Ins	Top 10 Race 15 min	How Google Builds the Perfect Team 20 min	Try a Check-In 40 min	Plan to Use a Check-In 10 min	Try the Habit 3 weeks	Partner Reflection 30 min
DURATION: 1 MONTH						
PROJECT HABIT: We Kick Off Work	The Great Kick-Off 15 min	Why Kick-Offs Matter 20 min	Role Play Kick-Off 35 min	Plan to Kick Off Work 15 min	Try the Habit 3 weeks	Quadrant Reflection 30 min
DURATION: 1 MONTH						

You Are Here

Why Does Responsive Learning Matter?

For responsive teams, learning is the engine that drives progress, effectiveness, and innovation. In education we use the word "learning" dozens of times a day but don't often pause to think about what it takes to support people, especially our adult staff, as learners.

For us, learning is intricately linked with curiosity, questions, mistakes, feedback, reflection, and sharing. The learning habit in this chapter specifically focuses on how to build a culture that encourages and supports your teammates to be learners.

Inspiration From The New School Rules

> " Ironically, while we're immersed in learning environments, many of us have not made a culture of learning central to our vision for our staff and school communities. Yet we've found over and over again, and research supports, that successful learning isn't about students alone. It's about entire organizations. "

Learning Habit: We Talk About Mistakes

This chapter will guide you through the five steps of The SEPAD Method—Spark, Expand, Practice, Apply, and Debrief—using the specific activities below to build the Learning Habit: We Talk About Mistakes.

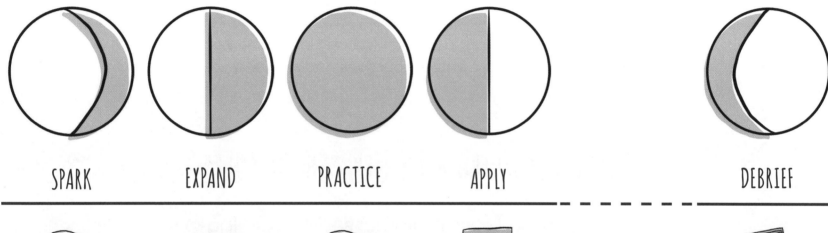

SPARK	EXPAND	PRACTICE	APPLY		DEBRIEF
Mr. Whiskers	Psychological Safety	Triad Share	Plan to Talk About Mistakes	Try the Habit	Reflect and Share
15 min	35 min	25 min	10 min	3 weeks	30 min

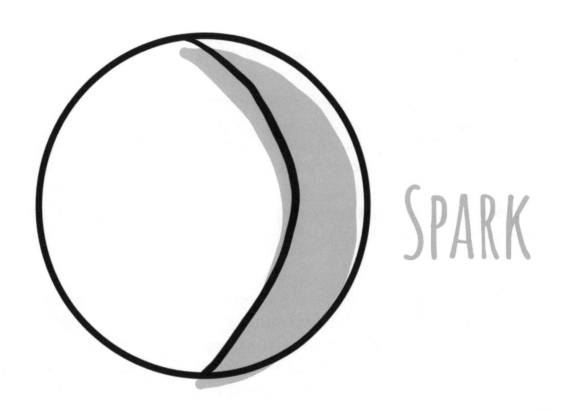

SPARK

SPARK: Mr. Whiskers

 13 Minutes    Interact as a Team

Why do you need new team habits for learning? We have found that although schools and districts support student learning, we often expect perfection from our adult staff and are uncomfortable making or witnessing mistakes. Making and talking about mistakes are essential for learning.

Play this short game to experience firsthand what it feels like to learn and make a mistake in the presence of others. We recommend playing for 5 minutes and debriefing for 5 minutes.

Mr. Whiskers is adapted from Play on Purpose. Learn more and see a video of the game in action at www.newteamhabits.com/learning#spark.

1. Form a circle.
2. One person leads by making eye contact with someone across the circle and saying, "Mr. Whiskers," to pass to that person. Practice a quick round with this prompt first so that people get the hang of it.
3. Then layer on the next two directional prompts. If you want to pass to the left, you say "Mista Vista." If you want to pass to the right, you say "Whiskey Mixer." (Yes, it's meant to be a tongue twister.)
4. Play using all three directional prompts. If you make a mistake (either you wait too long or you say the wrong thing), celebrate the mistake by shouting "Woo hoo!" and then run a lap around the circle back to your spot. The game can continue while you run your lap.
5. Play a few rounds. See how long or fast the group can go.
6. Before you return to your seats, debrief as a group about the experience of this game. How did it feel to make a mistake in front of this group? What made it easier or harder to make or witness a mistake? How does this relate to making mistakes in real life?

IDEAS SPARKED FROM MR. WHISKERS

 2 MINUTES    WRITE ON YOUR OWN

Once back at your seat, take 2 minutes to jot notes on your own regarding any ideas or insights sparked by Mr. Whiskers and your team discussion.

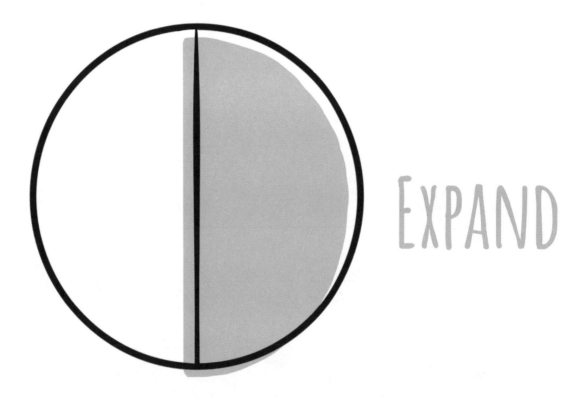

EXPAND

" Success can only be achieved through repeated failure
and introspection. In fact, success represents the
1 percent of your work which results from the
99 percent that is called failure. "

—Soichiro Honda, founder of Honda Motor Company

EXPAND: Psychological Safety

 15 Minutes    Watch as a Team

If we want to create a culture of learning and develop a growth mindset in our team members, we need to nurture an environment in which individuals are safe to share both learnings and failures. As we shared in **The NEW School Rules,** "In education, the stakes are so high that we do everything to avoid failure ... but failure is already happening, no? All learning means practice, errors, failure, and success, with steps forward and backward." The concept of psychological safety is core to creating a culture of responsive learning, where team members are safe to ask questions, admit mistakes, and learn from failures.

As a team, watch Harvard professor Amy Edmondson's 12-minute TEDx Talk on psychological safety using the link below. Take notes on the next page to prepare for a group activity to process your key takeaways on psychological safety.

www.newteamhabits.com/learning#expand

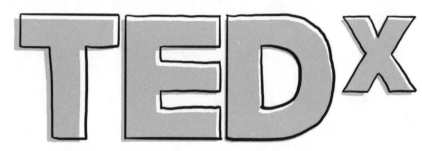

Take Notes During Video

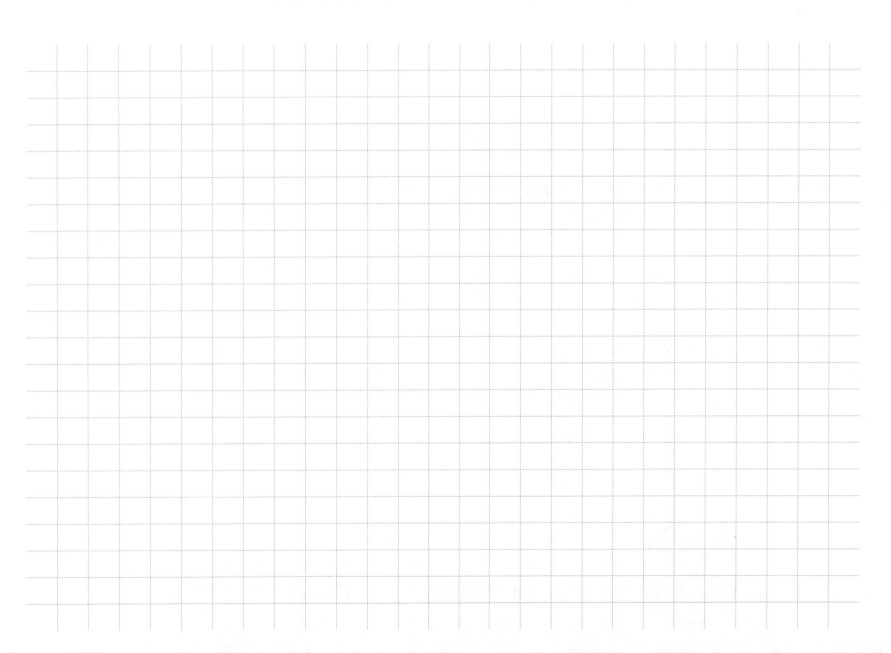

Learn the Habit: We Talk About Mistakes

 1 Minute    Read on Your Own

As Amy Edmondson shares, there are a few key ways that leaders can develop psychological safety with their teams:

1. **Frame the work as a learning problem.**
    "We've never been here before; we can't know what will happen; we've got to have everybody's brains and voices in the game."

2. **Acknowledge your own fallibility.**
    "I may miss something, I need to hear from you."

3. **Model curiosity.**
    "Every time we withhold, we rob ourselves and our colleagues of small moments of learning."

Of these three recommendations, we focused on the specific habit that we believe is most important to start modeling vulnerability and developing psychological safety.

WE TALK ABOUT MISTAKES TO MODEL VULNERABILITY
SO THAT OUR TEAM LEARNS AND GROWS TOGETHER

Team Activity: Visualize Key Concepts

 18 Minutes    Interact as a Team

Complete this activity to ensure your team understands the key concepts of Amy Edmondson's research and the importance of the Learning Habit: We Talk About Mistakes.

1. Break into groups of two to four people. Give each group a piece of poster paper and a marker (1 min)
2. As a group, create a visual poster (with no or few words) that answers the following questions: (8 min)
   a. What is psychological safety?
   b. How does talking about mistakes support psychological safety?
   c. Why does this matter for our team to be able to learn and grow together?

3. Give each group 30–60 seconds to share their poster. (4 min)
4. After all groups have shared, discuss as a whole team: Are there any key themes or key differences we are seeing across the groups? (5 min)

This Habit Is Working When . . .

 1 Minute    Read on Your Own

YOU ARE

- Talking about mistakes in one-on-one and team settings
- Making connections between your own learning and the learning of others on your team
- Trying new things with less fear

YOUR TEAM IS

- Asking more questions in one-on-one and team settings
- Talking about their own mistakes in one-on-one and team settings
- Pursuing new learnings and sharing with the team

Continue Expanding Your Knowledge

 Afterward    Read on Your Own

If you want to continue building your knowledge of psychological safety and modeling vulnerability, check out the following activities and resources on your own (outside of this team session):

Visit www.newteamhabits.com/learning#expand to access these resources and more.

1. Check out other teams' visuals. You can upload your team's visuals too!
2. Read the New York Times article, "Talking About Failure Is Crucial for Growth."
3. Share your ideas and insights about the Learning Habit: We Talk About Mistakes on Twitter with #teamhabits.

PRACTICE

How Will We Practice Talking About Mistakes?

You have recorded some ideas and learnings in the SPARK and EXPAND pages. Now it's time to PRACTICE before taking this habit out into the real world. We like triad sharing as a way to create meaningful space for conversation and feedback. Each triad group should use a timer to ensure that all three group members have time to share and get feedback before the whole group comes back together to make a plan to APPLY this habit in their day-to-day work.

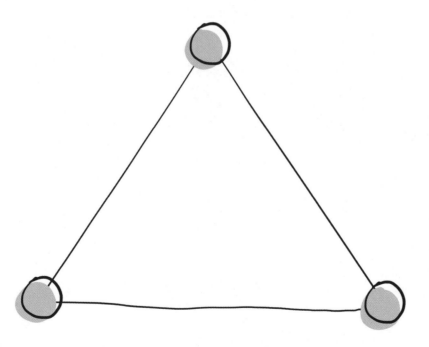

Prepare to Share

 5 Minutes    Write on Your Own

Use the space below to prepare what you're going to share in your triad group. What is an upcoming opportunity for you to talk about a mistake in a way that models vulnerability for others? This could be in a one-on-one or group setting. Write down what you might actually do or say so that you can get specific feedback from your triad group.

Try the Habit | Triad Share

 20 Minutes    Interact as a Team

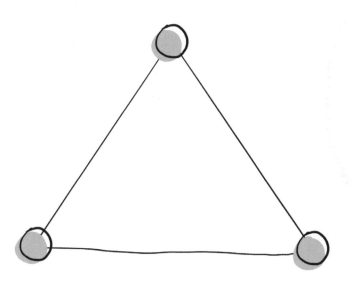

TRIAD SETUP

2 min: Get into triad groups (three people) and assign each person a number: #1, #2, #3.

TRIAD SHARE

1 min: #1 shares, #2 + #3 listen only

3 min: #2 + #3 share feedback, #1 takes notes

1 min: #1 shares takeaways from feedback

1 min: transition to next round

Repeat Triad Share protocol for each team member: 3 × 6 min = 18 min

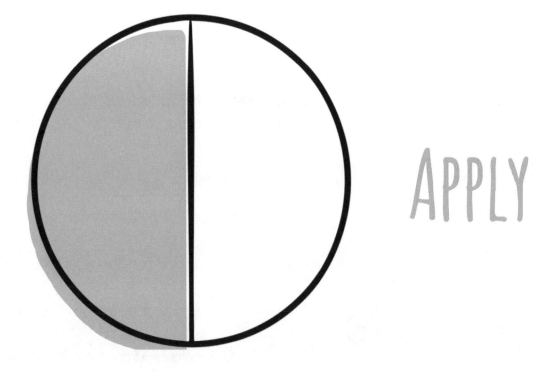

APPLY

" Take chances, make mistakes. That's how you grow.
Pain nourishes your courage. You have to fail in order
to practice being brave. "

—Mary Tyler Moore, actress

Commit to Try the Habit

 5 Minutes    Write on Your Own

Based on your learning today and the plan you shared with your triad group, commit to specific actions to try the Learning Habit: We Talk About Mistakes over the next 3 weeks. Add specific details regarding who, what, when, where, and how.

WHO	WHAT	WHEN	WHERE	HOW

Share Your Commitment With the Team

 4 Minutes    Interact as a Team

Our final activity of this session is to share our commitments. The goal of this activity is to close out our team session and to encourage team members to support each other with their commitments.

- Each person should share briefly (30 seconds).
- We recommend that as each person shares, one person records the person's name and a reminder of their commitment on a sticky note. One person per sticky note.
- Keep these sticky notes displayed on a wall or chart paper in a place that can serve as inspiration for the team over the next 3 weeks of application.

Go Try It! You Have 3 Weeks . . .

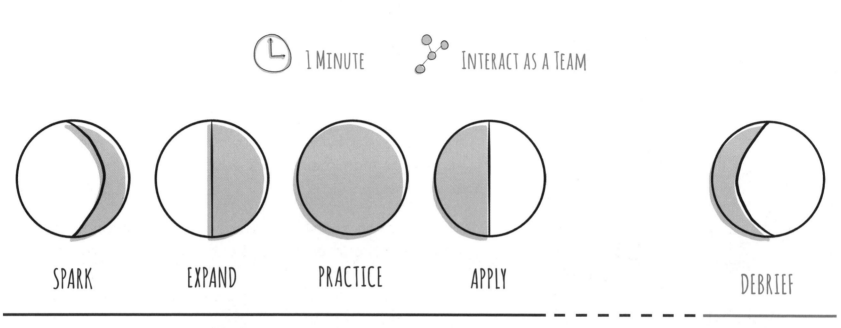

🕐 1 Minute   ⚲ Interact as a Team

SPARK	EXPAND	PRACTICE	APPLY		DEBRIEF

TEAM SESSION	TRY THE HABIT	TEAM SESSION
90 minutes to Spark, Expand, Practice, and Apply	3 weeks	30 minutes to Debrief

We're coming back together on _____ to debrief.

insert date/time based on training plan

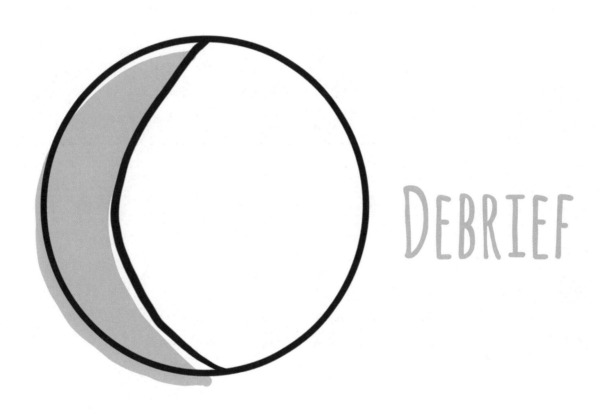

DEBRIEF

WHERE ARE WE IN THE TRAINING PLAN?

You've had the opportunity to try the Learning Habit: We Talk About Mistakes in the real world. The goal of today's team session is to share learnings and create a plan for making this habit stick moving forward.

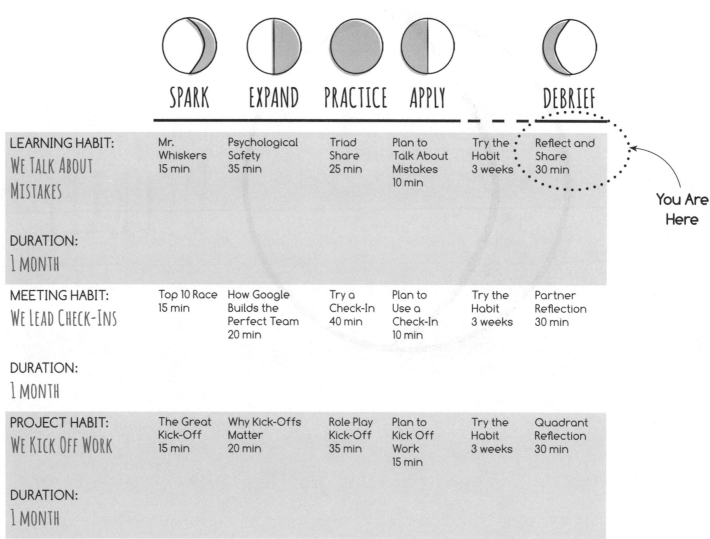

	SPARK	EXPAND	PRACTICE	APPLY		DEBRIEF
LEARNING HABIT: **We Talk About Mistakes** **DURATION:** 1 MONTH	Mr. Whiskers 15 min	Psychological Safety 35 min	Triad Share 25 min	Plan to Talk About Mistakes 10 min	Try the Habit 3 weeks	Reflect and Share 30 min
MEETING HABIT: **We Lead Check-Ins** **DURATION:** 1 MONTH	Top 10 Race 15 min	How Google Builds the Perfect Team 20 min	Try a Check-In 40 min	Plan to Use a Check-In 10 min	Try the Habit 3 weeks	Partner Reflection 30 min
PROJECT HABIT: **We Kick Off Work** **DURATION:** 1 MONTH	The Great Kick-Off 15 min	Why Kick-Offs Matter 20 min	Role Play Kick-Off 35 min	Plan to Kick Off Work 15 min	Try the Habit 3 weeks	Quadrant Reflection 30 min

You Are Here

You May Have Felt . . . .

 1 Minute  Read on Your Own

As you practiced the Learning Habit: We Talk About Mistakes, it is possible that you felt some of the following emotions:

- Fear about what your colleagues or teammates might think after you share a mistake
- Pride when a team member told you it was helpful to hear about your mistakes and learnings
- Distraction with all of the other work you have outside of practicing this habit
- Comfort in knowing that other members of this team are practicing the same habit

On the next page, you'll have an opportunity to reflect on what you tried and how you felt over the past 3 weeks.

DEBRIEF: Reflect on Your Own

 5 Minutes    Write on Your Own

You've tried the Learning Habit: We Talk About Mistakes (more than once, we hope!) over the past 3 weeks. Use the guiding questions below to reflect on your own. This reflection will prepare you to reflect and share as a team.

What did you commit to try?

What did you actually try?

What supported you?

What was difficult?

What was the impact?

Share Reflections as a Group

 15 Minutes    Interact as a Team

One of the greatest benefits of building this habit as a team is that you have other people to learn from and share with.

Take 15 minutes as a group to share reflections. You might go question by question through the reflections on the preceding page or have a more open, organic conversation. The goal is to learn and share beyond your own individual experience.

This group discussion will inspire your key takeaways on the next page.

Making the Habit Stick

 2 Minutes  Write on Your Own

Now that you've debriefed as a team, take 2 minutes to write yourself a note with any key takeaways you have for practicing this and other habits (e.g., practice the habit during an already scheduled meeting versus adding in a new meeting; have a buddy to check in with each week). Think of this like a reminder to yourself that you can come back to as you build other habits.

Commit to Try the Habit (Again and Again)

 5 Minutes    Write on Your Own

Based on your application over the past 3 weeks and the team reflection today, commit to the following specific actions to continue building the Learning Habit: We Talk About Mistakes.

Share the Habit!

 Afterward    Read on Your Own

If you want to share your individual and team learnings about building this learning habit, check out the following activities and resources on your own (outside of this team session):

Visit **www.newteamhabits.com/learning#debrief** to access all of these resources.

1. Share your learnings with another team you work with via an e-mail, as part of a newsletter, or in an upcoming conversation or meeting.
2. Connect with others who are practicing this habit on Twitter with #teamhabits.
3. Snap a photo of your reflection page and upload it to our website. Check out other teams' reflections too!

What Comes Next?

 1 Minute  Interact as a Team

Congratulations! You've just completed your first cycle of The SEPAD Method to build team habits. Here's what to do next:

1. Celebrate! Update your learning plan to record this milestone. Give each other a high-five. Seriously!
2. Share with someone outside of this team. Think of yourself as a spark for spreading this habit to other teams.
3. Start building your next team habit. Before you leave today, update your team's learning plan regarding any shifts in dates or times. Record the date and time for your next team session below.

We're coming back together on _____ for
insert date/time based on training plan

our 90-min team session on Meeting Habit: We Lead Check-Ins.

CHAPTER 4

MEETING HABIT:
WE LEAD CHECK-INS

The NEW School Power Rules
for Meeting Habits

Meetings are a place where we can practice responsive habits by building trust, distributing authority, and clarifying decision making. If you want additional context on responsive meetings and these two power rules, we recommend revisiting the original chapters in the book or visiting www.newschoolrules.com.

Build Trust and Allow Authority to Spread

**RULE #2
TEAMING**

Meetings are a place to build trust and practice working together as a team.

- Use meeting protocols to distribute authority and provide more equal participation and talk time across the team.
- Think of meetings as a space to practice how your team communicates, learns, collaborates, and makes decisions.

Aim for "Safe Enough to Try" Instead of Consensus

**RULE #4
DECISION
MAKING**

Meetings are a place to model "safe enough to try" and clear decision-making processes.

- Use meetings to focus on making decisions instead of defaulting to sharing information.
- Focus on whether decisions are "safe enough to try" instead of holding out for consensus.

WHERE ARE WE IN THE TRAINING PLAN?

We are in the second of three habit-building cycles. We will follow the same steps for building a team meeting habit that we did for building a team learning habit.

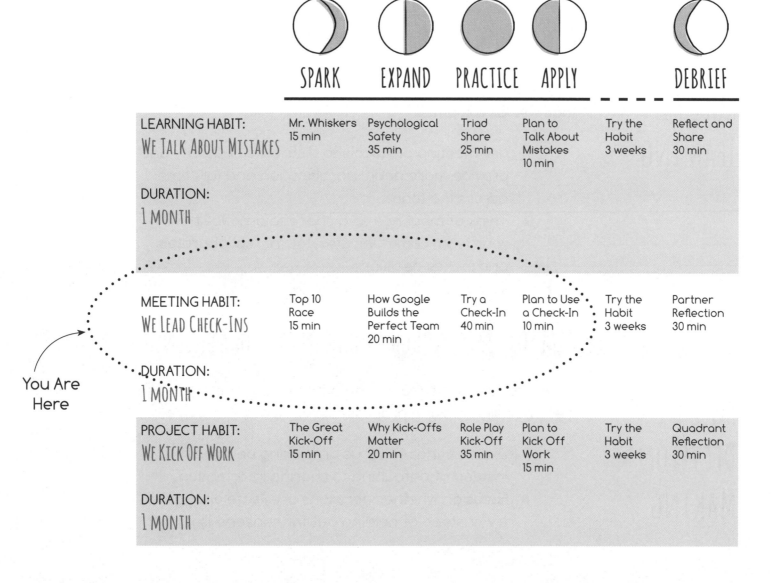

	SPARK	EXPAND	PRACTICE	APPLY		DEBRIEF
LEARNING HABIT: We Talk About Mistakes	Mr. Whiskers 15 min	Psychological Safety 35 min	Triad Share 25 min	Plan to Talk About Mistakes 10 min	Try the Habit 3 weeks	Reflect and Share 30 min
DURATION: 1 MONTH						
MEETING HABIT: We Lead Check-Ins	Top 10 Race 15 min	How Google Builds the Perfect Team 20 min	Try a Check-In 40 min	Plan to Use a Check-In 10 min	Try the Habit 3 weeks	Partner Reflection 30 min
DURATION: 1 MONTH						
PROJECT HABIT: We Kick Off Work	The Great Kick-Off 15 min	Why Kick-Offs Matter 20 min	Role Play Kick-Off 35 min	Plan to Kick Off Work 15 min	Try the Habit 3 weeks	Quadrant Reflection 30 min
DURATION: 1 MONTH						

You Are Here

Why Do Responsive Meetings Matter?

For many of us, meetings occupy the majority of our work day. Meetings have the potential to be powerful levers for sharing and collaboration but unfortunately are often disengaging and inefficient.

We have found that meetings are a powerful place to change the way we engage and work with each other. By shifting the way you start your meetings, you can change the tone, engagement, and ultimately culture of your meetings and your team.

Inspiration From The New School Rules

66 You might balk at taking turns to speak in meetings and waiting for your turn. If you are one of the people who has no problem speaking up, it might feel silly. However, consider the person who hasn't been comfortable speaking up during meetings who may feel liberated by the structure. These quieter team members might finally feel they have a safe space to contribute. 99

Meeting Habit: We Lead Check-Ins

This chapter will guide you through the five steps of The SEPAD Method—Spark, Expand, Practice, Apply, and Debrief—using the specific activities below to build the Meeting Habit: We Lead Check-Ins.

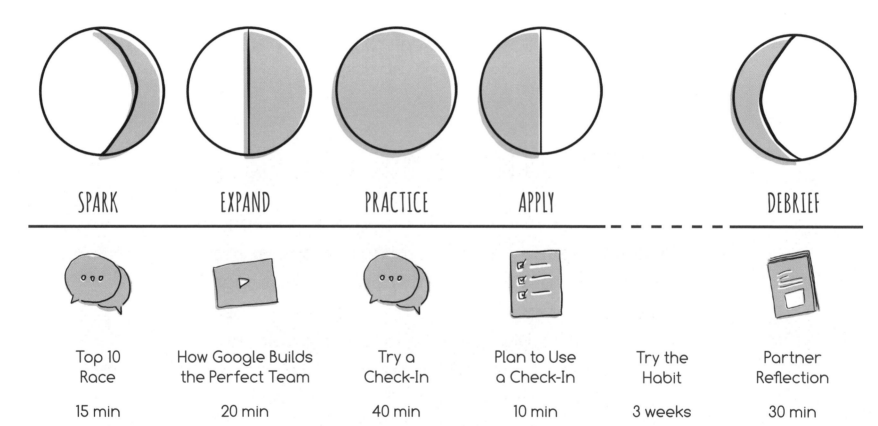

SPARK	EXPAND	PRACTICE	APPLY		DEBRIEF
Top 10 Race	How Google Builds the Perfect Team	Try a Check-In	Plan to Use a Check-In	Try the Habit	Partner Reflection
15 min	20 min	40 min	10 min	3 weeks	30 min

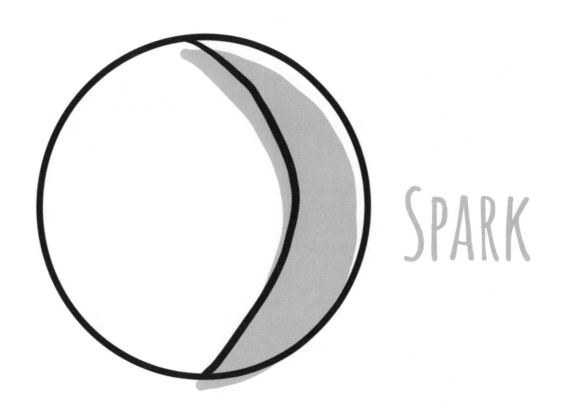

SPARK

SPARK: Top 10 Race

 5 Minutes    Interact as a Team

This spark activity is inspired by David Letterman's classic late-night talk show Top 10 lists. See our compilation of Top 10 lists at www.newteamhabits.com/meeting#spark.

PREP FOR TOP 10 RACE

1. Break into groups of 2 or 3 people.
2. Prepare an upbeat song to play during the race to amp up the energy.

READY ... SET ... GO!

3. Start the race. Each group should list the top 10 team habits for disengaging at meetings.
4. Stop the race when the first group reaches 10.
5. Cheer for the winning group!

Top 10 Team Habits for Disengaging at Meetings
1.
2.
3.
4.
5.
6.
7.
8.
9.
10.

WHAT DOES THIS MEAN FOR OUR MEETINGS?

 10 Minutes    Interact as a Team

1. Take 7–8 minutes as a full team to share:
   a. What habits for disengagement did your teams list in Top 10 Race?
   b. How do these habits for disengagement show up in our team meetings currently?
   c. What could be gained by increasing engagement at our meetings?

2. Take 1–2 minutes to capture key takeaways below:

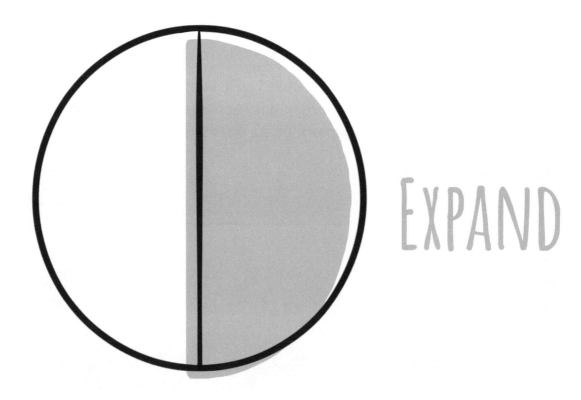

EXPAND

" Learn as if you were to live forever. "

—Mahatma Gandhi, Indian political
and civil rights leader

EXPAND: How Google Builds the Perfect Team

 5 Minutes    Interact as a Team

Google studied more than 200 teams as part of Project Aristotle to answer the question: What makes certain teams more effective than others? This video from Pulitzer Prize–winning journalist Charles Duhigg provides a summary of that study and key takeaways specifically around what highly effective teams do in meetings.

As a team, watch the 3-minute video "How Google Builds the Perfect Team," linked from the website below. Take notes on the next page to prepare for a group activity to process your key takeaways.

www.newteamhabits.com/meeting#expand

Take Notes During Video

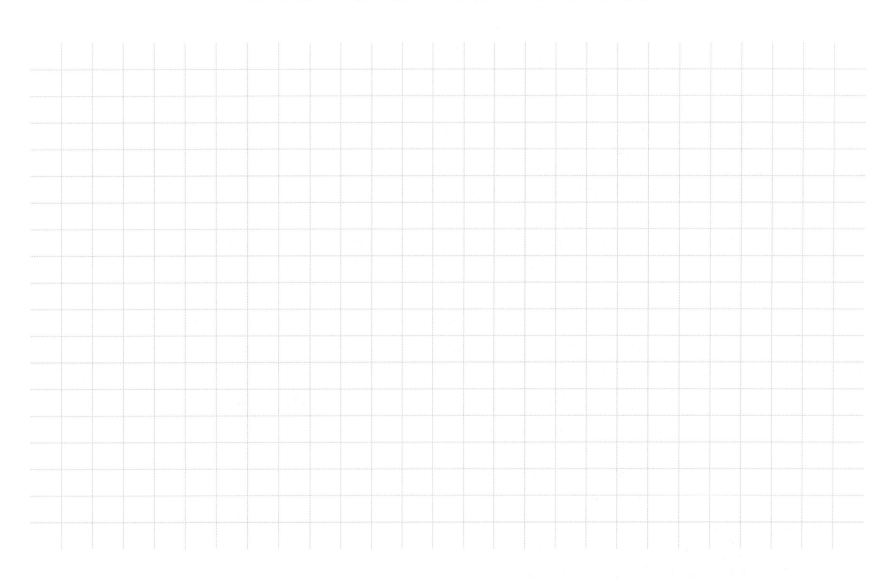

LEARN THE HABIT: WE LEAD CHECK-INS

 1 MINUTE    READ ON YOUR OWN

As Charles Duhigg shares, two key elements are present in the meetings of highly effective teams:

1. **Equality in Conversational Turn-Taking**

   "During a meeting, or a set of meetings, if everyone speaks at roughly the same amount, then that team is much more likely to succeed."

2. **Ostentatious Listening**

   "In addition to encouraging you to talk more, I as a team leader or team member have to show you that I'm listening by doing things like repeating what you just told me or closing my computer so I can make eye contact with you."

The way your team starts a meeting has a tremendous impact on how your team is able to embody the above practices. We recommend the specific habit of leading a check-in to start a meeting as an entry point for encouraging equality in conversational turn-taking and ostentatious listening.

 WE LEAD CHECK-INS TO INCREASE PRESENCE SO THAT OUR TEAM HAS MORE ENGAGEMENT AND EQUAL TALK TIME IN MEETINGS

Team Activity: Watch Team Check-In + Debrief

 13 Minutes  Interact as a Team

Check-ins provide an opening activity to increase presence and engagement at meetings.

1. Watch the 3-min video of a team check-in at www.newteamhabits.com/meeting#expand.
2. Take 10 min to share as a team:
   a. How did the check-in support conversational turn-taking and ostentatious listening?
   b. What did you like about this team's check-in?
   c. What do you want to remember as you practice leading your own team check-ins today?

TIPS FOR CHECK-INS	SAMPLE CHECK-IN QUESTIONS
1. Check-ins should be led by a facilitator, someone who keeps the sharing flowing.	• How are you feeling coming into this meeting?
2. During check-ins, the team should be seated for easy eye contact and tech should be set aside.	• What is occupying your mind as you enter this meeting?
3. The facilitator should have one volunteer start and flow in a "whip around," ensuring everyone has a sacred space to share without interruption.	• How do you feel on a scale of 1–5? • What color represents how you feel right now?
4. Each check-in should be 60 seconds or less.	• What's the best thing that's happened to you today?

This Habit Is Working When . . .

 1 Minute    Read on Your Own

YOU ARE

- Fully present at the start of meetings
- Getting to know your teammates in a deeper way through check-in questions
- Engaging in conversational turn-taking during meetings

YOUR TEAM IS

- Fully present at the start of meetings
- Deepening relationships and trust through check-in questions
- Sharing talk time more equally in meetings

CONTINUE EXPANDING YOUR KNOWLEDGE

 AFTERWARD  READ ON YOUR OWN

If you want to continue building your knowledge of responsive meetings, conversational turn-taking, and ostentatious listening, check out the following activities and resources on your own (outside of this team session):

Visit www.newteamhabits.com/meeting#expand to access all of these resources.

1. Explore additional ideas for check-in questions.
2. Read "How to Increase Focus at Your Meetings."
3. Read Atlassian's "Running Effective Meetings: A Guide for Humans."
4. Read the New York Times article, "What Google Learned From the Quest to Build a Perfect Team."
5. Share your ideas and insights about the Meeting Habit: We Lead Check-Ins on Twitter with #teamhabits.

PRACTICE

How Will We Practice Leading Check-Ins?

🕐 1 Minute   ⚛ Read on Your Own

You have recorded some ideas and learnings in the SPARK and EXPAND pages. Now it's time to PRACTICE before taking this habit out into the real world. The best way to practice leading a check-in is to do it. You will go through three practice rounds of checking in as a full team before making an individual plan to APPLY this habit in one or more of your upcoming meetings.

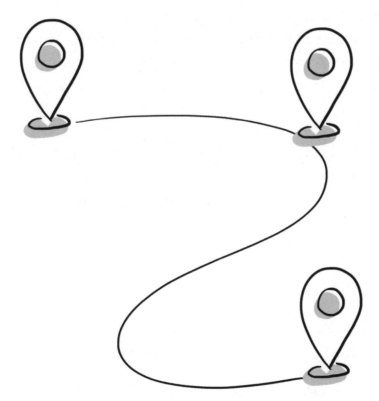

Prepare to Lead a Check-In

 5 Minutes    Interact as a Team

Fill in the first two columns in the table below to prepare for three quick whole-team practice rounds of check-ins. After each check-in practice, you will debrief as a group in preparation for the next practice round.

1. Decide who will be the facilitator for each practice round. You might have the same facilitator each time or give a new person a chance to practice each round.
2. Decide on the check-in question for each practice round. You can find some of our favorite check-in questions on page 91 and at www.newteamhabits.com/meeting#practice.

Take notes in the far-right column below, after each check-in round practice.

	Facilitator	Check-In Question	Notes From Debrief
Example	Carla	What is occupying your mind as we start this meeting?	Tech distractions: Put down all tech for our next practice round.
ROUND #1			
ROUND #2			
ROUND #3			

Try the Habit | Check-In Rounds

 30 Minutes  Interact as a Team

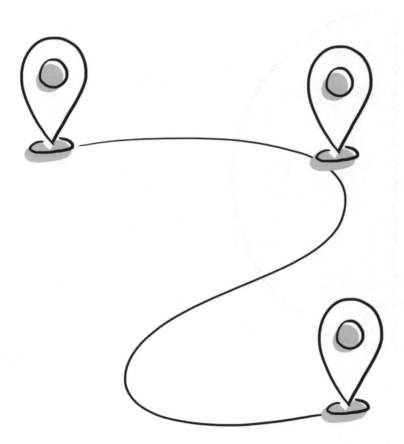

ROUND 1

4 min: Practice Check-In #1

6 min: Debrief Check-In #1

ROUND 2

4 min: Practice Check-In #2

6 min: Debrief Check-In #2

ROUND 3

4 min: Practice Check-In #3

6 min: Debrief Check-In #3

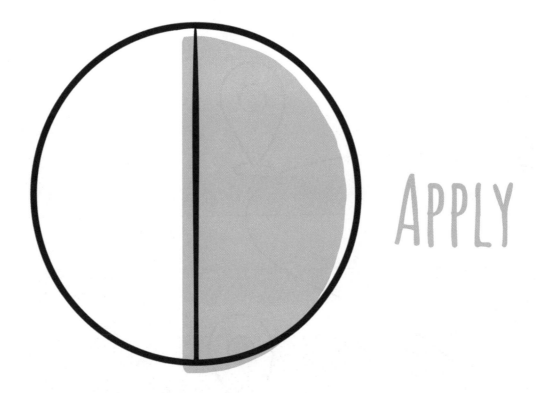

APPLY

" Knowledge is of no value unless
you put it into practice. "

—Anton Chekhov, Russian playwright

Commit to Try the Habit

 4 Minutes    Write on Your Own

Based on your learning and practice today, commit to trying the Meeting Habit: We Lead Check-Ins at some of your upcoming meetings. We recommend trying at least five check-ins over the 3 weeks before this group comes back together to debrief. This will give you a variety of experiences and examples to share from.

	Meeting	Check-In Question	Why Do I Want to Try This Question With This Group?
Example	District cabinet	What is occupying your mind as we start this meeting?	This team often brings a lot of distractions and worries into our meeting, and I'd love to be able to name and share them, and then move forward.
Check-In #1			
Check-In #2			
Check-In #3			
Check-In #4			
Check-In #5			

Share Your Commitment With the Team

 5 Minutes  Interact as a Team

Our final activity of this session is to share our commitments. The goal of this activity is to close out this team session and to encourage team members to support each other with their commitments.

- Share one of your commitments to trying a check-in (no need to share all five!).
- Each person should share briefly (30 seconds).
- If you notice someone has a similar commitment, make a plan to connect during the 3-week application period.

Go Try It! You Have 3 Weeks . . .

 1 Minute    Interact as a Team

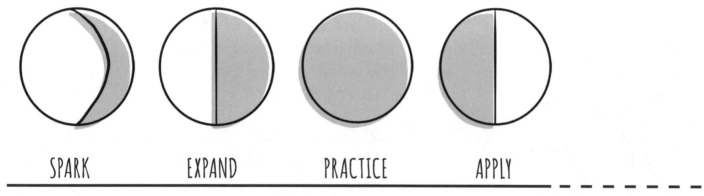

| SPARK | EXPAND | PRACTICE | APPLY | | DEBRIEF |

| | TEAM SESSION | | | TRY THE HABIT | TEAM SESSION |
| | 90 minutes to Spark, Expand, Practice, and Apply | | | 3 weeks | 30 minutes to Debrief |

We're coming back together on _____ to debrief.

insert date/time based on training plan

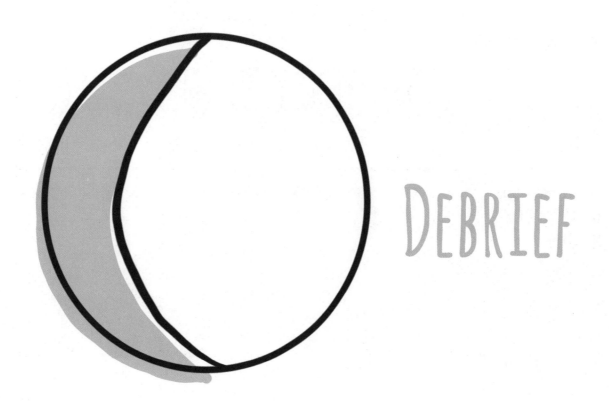

DEBRIEF

Where Are We in the Training Plan?

You've had the opportunity to try the Meeting Habit: We Lead Check-Ins in the real world. The goal of today's team session is to share learnings and create a plan for making this habit stick moving forward.

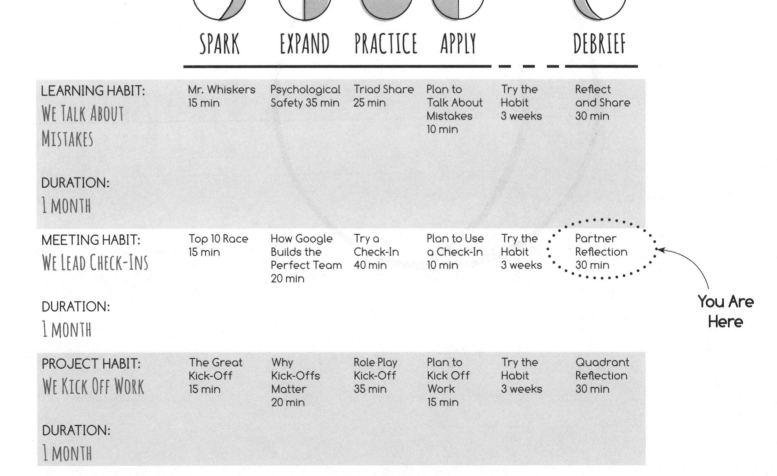

	SPARK	EXPAND	PRACTICE	APPLY		DEBRIEF
LEARNING HABIT: We Talk About Mistakes	Mr. Whiskers 15 min	Psychological Safety 35 min	Triad Share 25 min	Plan to Talk About Mistakes 10 min	Try the Habit 3 weeks	Reflect and Share 30 min
DURATION: 1 MONTH						
MEETING HABIT: We Lead Check-Ins	Top 10 Race 15 min	How Google Builds the Perfect Team 20 min	Try a Check-In 40 min	Plan to Use a Check-In 10 min	Try the Habit 3 weeks	Partner Reflection 30 min
DURATION: 1 MONTH						
PROJECT HABIT: We Kick Off Work	The Great Kick-Off 15 min	Why Kick-Offs Matter 20 min	Role Play Kick-Off 35 min	Plan to Kick Off Work 15 min	Try the Habit 3 weeks	Quadrant Reflection 30 min
DURATION: 1 MONTH						

You Are Here

YOU MAY HAVE FELT . . . .

 1 MINUTE    READ ON YOUR OWN

As you practiced the Meeting Habit: We Lead Check-Ins, it is possible that you felt some of the following emotions:

- Stress about remembering to do "one more thing" in your meetings
- Satisfaction as you saw check-ins start to shift the culture of and engagement in your meetings
- Indecision in selecting the right check-in question for each meeting
- Relief in knowing that you have five (or more!) opportunities to practice the check-ins and that you don't have to be perfect the first time

On the next page, you'll have an opportunity to reflect on what you tried and how you felt over the past 3 weeks.

DEBRIEF: Reflect on Your Own

 5 Minutes  Write on Your Own

You've tried the Meeting Habit: We Lead Check-Ins five or more times over the past 3 weeks. Use the guiding questions below to reflect on your own. This reflection will prepare you to debrief and share as a team.

What was your most successful check-in?

What was your least successful check-in?

What was the biggest impact of leading check-ins?

Share Reflections With a Partner

 10 Minutes    Interact as a Team

One of the greatest benefits of building this habit as a team is that you have other people to learn from and share with.

Take 10 minutes to share reflections with a partner. You might go question by question through the reflections on the preceding page or have a more open, organic conversation. The goal is to learn and share beyond your own individual experience.

This partner sharing will inspire your key takeaways on the next page.

Making the Habit Stick

 2 Minutes    Write on Your Own

Now that you've debriefed with a partner, take 2 minutes to write yourself a note with any key takeaways you have for practicing this and other habits. Revisit your key takeaways from page 72 in Chapter 3. What is consistent? What new learnings do you have about how you might make this habit stick?

Commit to Try the Habit (Again and Again)

 10 Minutes    Interact as a Team

As a team, process the learnings and insights from your partner reflections. Commit to how you want to continue building the Meeting Habit: We Lead Check-Ins. This might be a team commitment, an individual commitment, or both.

SHARE THE HABIT!

 Afterward    Read on Your Own

If you want to share your individual and team learnings about building this meeting habit, check out the following activities and resources on your own (outside of this team session):

Visit www.newteamhabits.com/meeting#debrief to access all of these resources.

1. Share your learnings with another team you work with via an e-mail, as part of a newsletter, or in an upcoming conversation or meeting.
2. Connect with others who are practicing this habit on Twitter with #teamhabits.
3. Snap a photo of your reflection page and upload it to our website. Check out other teams' reflections too!

What Comes Next?

 1 Minute    Interact as a Team

Congratulations! You've just completed your second cycle of The SEPAD Method to build team habits. Here's what to do next:

1. Celebrate! Update your learning plan to record this milestone. Fist bump each other. Seriously!
2. Share with someone outside of this team. Think of yourself as a spark for spreading this habit to other teams.
3. Start building your next team habit. Before you leave today, update your team's learning plan regarding any shifts in dates or times. Record the date and time for your next team session below.

We're coming back together on _____ for

insert date/time based on training plan

our 90-min team session on Project Habit: We Kick Off Work.

CHAPTER 5

Project Habit:
We Kick Off Work

The NEW School Power Rules for Meeting Habits

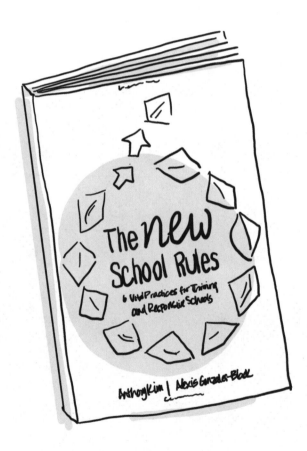

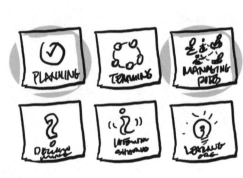

Projects offer an opportunity to practice planning and managing roles in a more responsive way. If you want additional context on responsive projects and these two power rules, we recommend revisiting the original chapters in the book or visiting www.newschoolrules.com.

Plan for Change, Not Perfection

**RULE #1
PLANNING**

Projects are an opportunity to practice planning for change with a clear purpose.

- Build learning time and pivot points into your project roadmap.
- Focus on the purpose of a project instead of the project plan to empower your team to learn and iterate.

Define the Work Before You Define the People

**RULE #3
MANAGING
ROLES**

Projects provide a focused space to practice new ways of defining roles and work on your team.

- Assign project responsibilities based on the work that needs to be done, not job titles.
- Focus on defining roles to ensure alignment and clarity in authority and decision making.

WHERE ARE WE IN THE TRAINING PLAN?

We are in the third of three habit-building cycles. We will follow the same steps for building a team project habit that we did for building a team learning habit and building a team meeting habit.

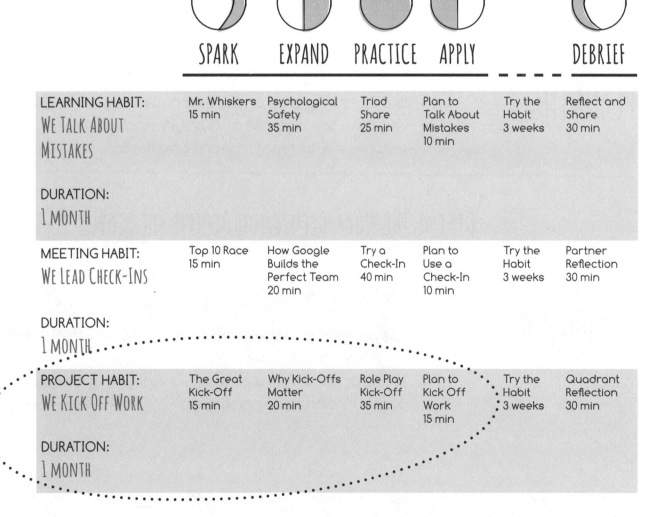

	SPARK	EXPAND	PRACTICE	APPLY		DEBRIEF
LEARNING HABIT: We Talk About Mistakes DURATION: 1 MONTH	Mr. Whiskers 15 min	Psychological Safety 35 min	Triad Share 25 min	Plan to Talk About Mistakes 10 min	Try the Habit 3 weeks	Reflect and Share 30 min
MEETING HABIT: We Lead Check-Ins DURATION: 1 MONTH	Top 10 Race 15 min	How Google Builds the Perfect Team 20 min	Try a Check-In 40 min	Plan to Use a Check-In 10 min	Try the Habit 3 weeks	Partner Reflection 30 min
PROJECT HABIT: We Kick Off Work DURATION: 1 MONTH	The Great Kick-Off 15 min	Why Kick-Offs Matter 20 min	Role Play Kick-Off 35 min	Plan to Kick Off Work 15 min	Try the Habit 3 weeks	Quadrant Reflection 30 min

You Are Here

Why Do Responsive Projects Matter?

Team projects are a part of our daily work. In fact, most districts have myriad projects happening at any given time. Yet we often launch into projects without clearly communicating the purpose, goals, roles, or roadmap.

By shifting the way you kick off work, both at the start of a project and during a project at the start of a new phase or sprint of work, you can begin to shift the way your team works together and refine the plan with greater speed and effectiveness to meet your project goal.

Inspiration from the New School Rules

66 Too often we get pulled into project teams where the purpose is assumed and unspoken. For example, you may be invited to a working group called Safety Task Force. The purpose isn't explicitly stated, but it's assumed that this group convenes to talk about safety issues. Weeks or months go by with meeting after meeting. Over time, little shifts go unnoticed, the team grows, and the work changes. One day you show up for yet another meeting and wonder why you are there, or it dawns on you that everyone is working toward different goals. Making assumptions about the purpose of a team, and not publishing or revisiting it, means that the goal fades into obscurity and the team wastes time and resources. Finding the right purpose, making it transparent, and reviewing it regularly can help teams move in the right direction and help individuals decide how they will contribute to the overall goal. 99

Project Habit: We Kick Off Work

This chapter will guide you through the five steps of The SEPAD Method—Spark, Expand, Practice, Apply, and Debrief—using the specific activities below to build the Project Habit: We Kick Off Work.

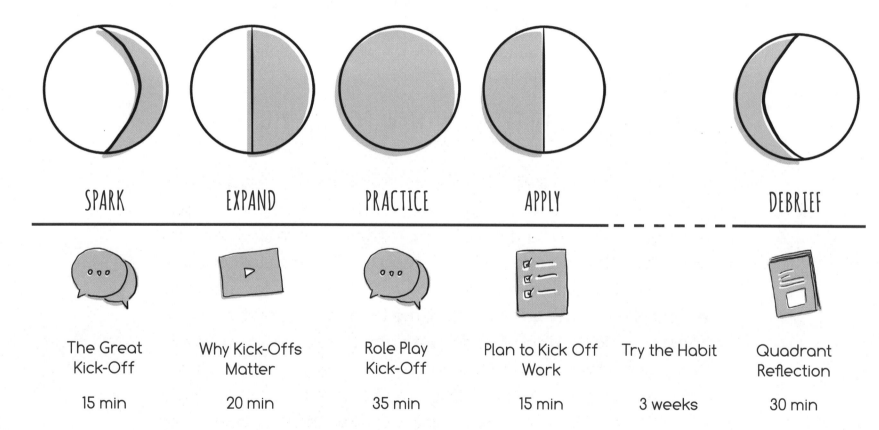

SPARK	EXPAND	PRACTICE	APPLY		DEBRIEF
The Great Kick-Off	Why Kick-Offs Matter	Role Play Kick-Off	Plan to Kick Off Work	Try the Habit	Quadrant Reflection
15 min	20 min	35 min	15 min	3 weeks	30 min

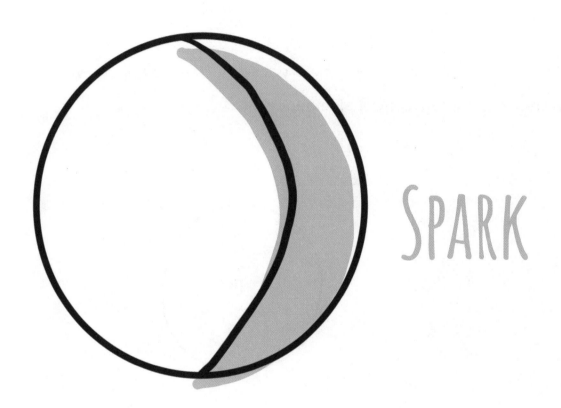

SPARK

SPARK: THE GREAT KICK-OFF

 5 Minutes    Interact as a Team

For this spark, watch the video "The Great Kick-Off" linked at
www.newteamhabits.com/project#spark.

WHAT DOES THIS MEAN FOR OUR PROJECT?

 10 Minutes   Interact as a Team

1. Take 7–8 minutes as a full team to discuss:
   a. What about this video resonated with your own kick-off experiences?
   b. What is the result of kicking off work in this way (or not kicking off work at all)?
   c. What could be gained by changing the way we kick off work?

2. Take 1–2 minutes to capture key takeaways below.

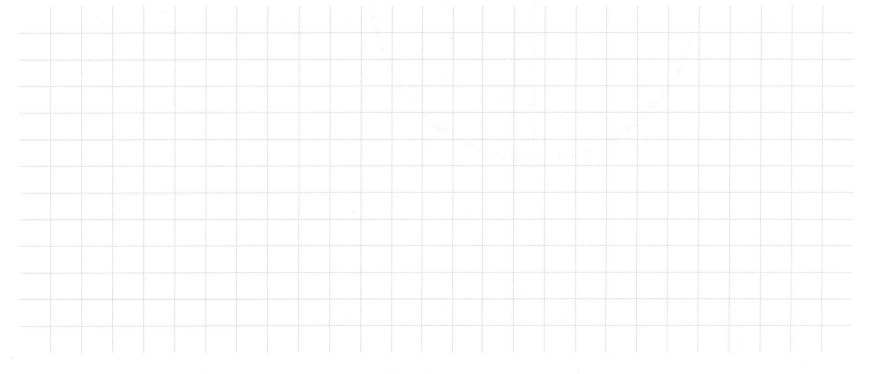

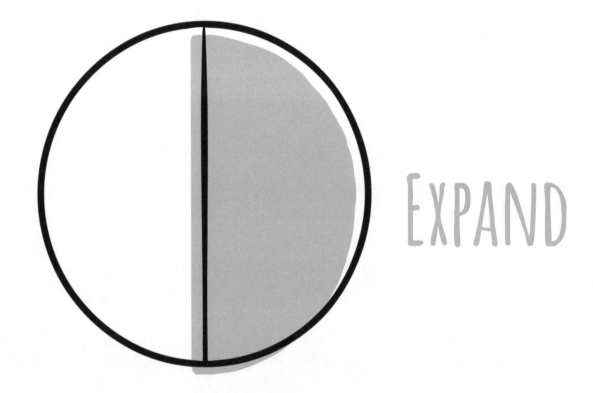

EXPAND

" Learning is not attained by chance, it must be sought with ardor and diligence. "

—Abigail Adams, former first lady

EXPAND: WHY KICK-OFFS MATTER

 8 MINUTES  READ ON YOUR OWN

Many leaders, thanks to the popularity of books such as Simon Sinek's **Start With Why,** have a great focus on the purpose of a project. However, few leaders take the time to communicate the purpose, the roles, and the roadmap that will support achieving the project's purpose.

The two articles linked from the website below will help your team reflect on the importance of kicking off work, whether an entire project or the next phase or sprint of work. We've specifically selected articles from organizations that are leading the way in thinking about project management and teamwork. Even though these resources in some cases focus on product design, we think they contain important lessons for education leaders.

1. Visit www.newteamhabits.com/project#expand to access the articles.
2. Take 5–7 minutes to read "Kicking Off: How to Start a Mission-Driven Team" and "Avoid These 5 Mistakes for an Amazing Kick-Off Meeting" on your own.
3. Take notes on the next page as you read to prepare for a team discussion on the page after that.

Take Notes During Reading

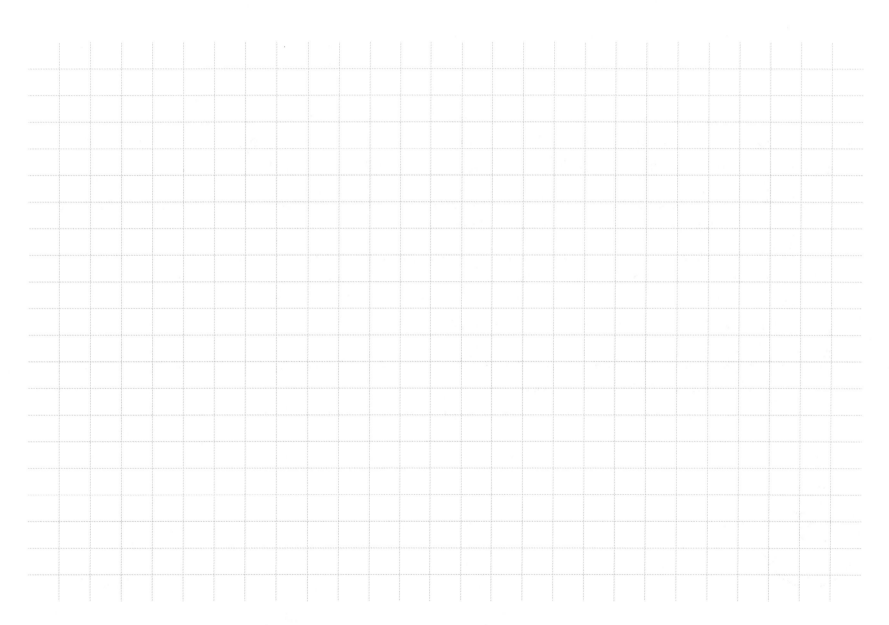

Learn the Habit: We Kick Off Work

 1 Minute    Read on Your Own

The two articles you read described how kicking off work provides the team with greater clarity on purpose, roles, and roadmap. This in turn provides the team with a better understanding of the work and greater context and agency to adjust the work plan as needed to meet the project's purpose.

1. As the Parabol team shares in "Kicking Off: How to Start a Mission-Driven Team," the articulation of a project's mission is critical in effectively kicking off work.

   "A team's mission is like its north star, it's the direction everybody will march even if there isn't a guarantee the team will reach it: Vasco de Gama circumnavigating the globe, Lewis and Clark reaching the Pacific, or Elon Musk colonizing Mars. A mission is useless if its members don't understand why it's important or what their role is on it."

2. As the Atlassian team shares in "Avoid These 5 Mistakes for an Amazing Kick-Off Meeting," a good kick-off meeting serves multiple purposes.

   "A good kick-off meeting will unite your project team with a shared understanding of what you're doing and why. It's a time to make decisions about how you'll work together (e.g., How will we communicate? How often will we meet?), map out a rough timeline, and call out risks."

WE KICK OFF WORK TO INCREASE CLARITY ON PURPOSE, ROLES, AND ROADMAP, SO THAT OUR TEAM IS MORE AGILE IN ADJUSTING OUR PLANS TO MEET OUR PURPOSE

Team Activity: Record Headlines

 10 Minutes  Interact as a Team

As a team, discuss your reflections from the two articles you read and the key takeaways. To help synthesize the why behind the Project Habit: We Kick Off Work, fill in this newspaper page with two headlines about why kicking off work matters.

The Why Kicking Off Work Matters Gazette

Headline 1

Headline 2

This Habit Is Working When . . .

 1 Minute    Read on Your Own

YOU ARE

- Articulating the why of every project
- Setting aside time to kick off work, whether new sprints, phases, or projects
- Seeing greater alignment and buy-in from your team in leading work

YOUR TEAM IS

- Clearer on the purpose, roles, and roadmap of work
- Starting to host its own kick-offs with other teams
- Able to act with more agility in adjusting the roles and roadmap of the work based on its purpose

Continue Expanding Your Knowledge

 Afterward  Read on Your Own

If you want to continue building your knowledge of responsive projects, and the purpose, roles, and roadmap for work, check out the following activities and resources on your own (outside of this team session):

Visit www.newteamhabits.com/project#expand to access all of these resources.

1. Explore additional ideas for kicking off work.
2. Read "The Importance of a Kick Off Meeting for High Value Partnerships."
3. Read "Sprinting: Working in Cycles."
4. Share your ideas and insights about the Project Habit: We Kick Off Work on Twitter with #teamhabits.

PRACTICE

How Will We Practice Kicking Off Work?

 1 Minute    Read on Your Own

You have recorded some ideas and learnings in the SPARK and EXPAND pages. Now it's time to PRACTICE before taking this habit out into the real world. The best way to practice leading a kick-off meeting is to do it. You will break into groups of four to practice leading a kick-off meeting before making an individual plan to APPLY this habit in one or more of your upcoming meetings.

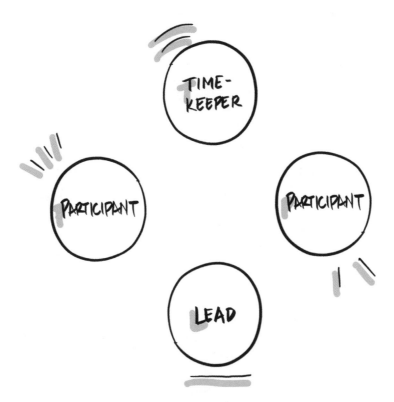

Prepare to Role Play a Kick-Off

 4 Minutes    Interact as a Team

Use the space below to reflect on a kick-off meeting you would like to lead in the real world. You will be role playing in teams of four. One person will practice kicking off today; however, we believe it is helpful for each person to prepare a kick-off as a frame for actively reflecting during the role play and as a first step for preparing for application in the real world.

WHAT WORK AM I LEADING THAT WOULD BENEFIT FROM A KICK-OFF MEETING? WHY?

WHAT IDEAS FROM OUR KNOWLEDGE BUILDING TODAY DO I WANT TO BRING INTO THIS KICK-OFF (E.G., ARTICULATE PURPOSE, DEFINE SUCCESS, BUILD RELATIONSHIPS, ALIGN ON ROLES, CREATE ROADMAP)?

Try the Habit | Role Play Kick-Off

 30 Minutes   Interact as a Team

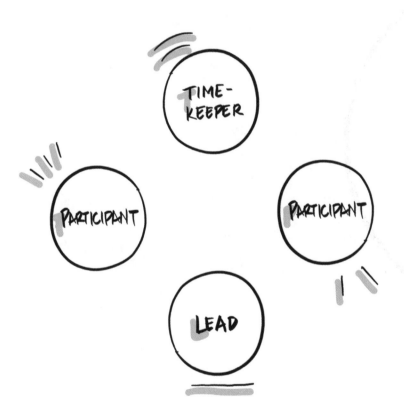

Roles for Kick-Off Meeting Role Play

- Lead (1): Leads role play kick-off meeting based on the planning from the preceding page.
- Participants (2): Participate in role play kick-off meeting by listening and asking questions; give feedback to the lead after the role play.
- Timekeeper (1): One of the participants; keeps track of time using guide below.

Timing for Kick-Off Meeting Role Play

- 5 min context sharing: Lead shares with participants the context for this kick-off.
- 5 min role play: Lead and participants role play the kick-off meeting.
- 15 min debrief: Participants share feedback with lead; lead processes insights and new ideas to take forward into real-world application.
- 5 min whole-group share: Team shares learnings and insights as a whole group.

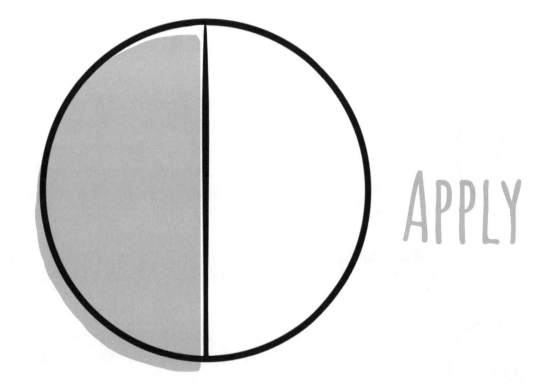

APPLY

" You don't learn to walk by following rules.
You learn by doing, and by falling over. "

—Richard Branson, founder of the Virgin Group

Commit to Try the Habit

 4 Minutes    Write on Your Own

Based on your learnings and practice today, commit to trying the Project Habit: We Kick Off Work. This could be a new project, a new phase of work, or a new work sprint. The goal is to create greater alignment, clarity, and ownership across your team.

Following the role play, what changes do I want to make to my plan to kick off work?
When and how do I plan to kick off the work?
What do I anticipate the impact of this kick-off to be on my team and our work?

Share Your Commitment With the Team

  Interact as a Team

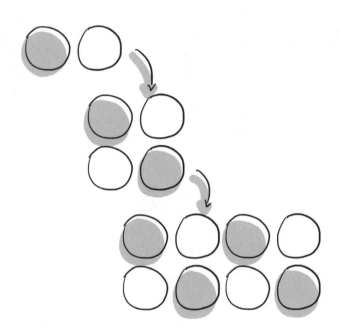

Our final activity of this session is to share our commitments. The goal of this activity is to close out this team session and to encourage team members to support each other with their commitments.

- Share your commitments to practice the Project Habit: We Kick Off Work using the Snowball Discussion Method.
- Start by sharing in pairs.
- After sharing in pairs, have two pairs join into groups of four people.
- Finally, have two groups of four join into a final group of eight for sharing.

Go Try It! You Have 3 Weeks . . .

 1 Minute    Interact as a Team

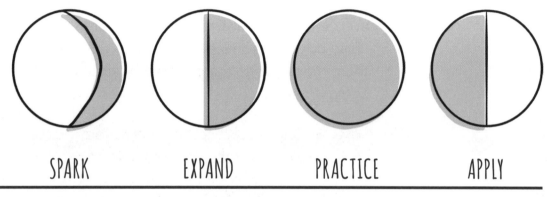

| SPARK | EXPAND | PRACTICE | APPLY | | DEBRIEF |

TEAM SESSION

90 minutes to
Spark, Expand, Practice, and Apply

TRY THE HABIT

3 weeks

TEAM SESSION

30 minutes to
Debrief

We're coming back together on _____ to debrief.

insert date/time based on training plan

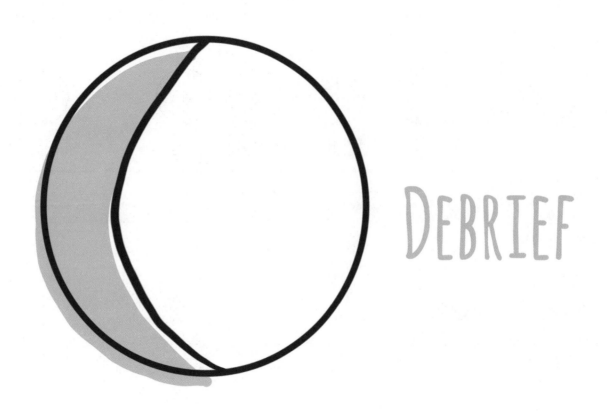

DEBRIEF

Where Are We in the Training Plan?

You've had the opportunity to try the Project Habit: We Kick Off Work. The goal of today's team session is to share learnings and create a plan for making this habit stick moving forward.

	SPARK	EXPAND	PRACTICE	APPLY		DEBRIEF
LEARNING HABIT: We Talk About Mistakes **DURATION:** 1 Month	Mr. Whiskers 15 min	Psychological Safety 35 min	Triad Share 25 min	Plan to Talk About Mistakes 10 min	Try the Habit 3 weeks	Reflect and Share 30 min
MEETING HABIT: We Lead Check-Ins **DURATION:** 1 Month	Top 10 Race 15 min	How Google Builds the Perfect Team 20 min	Try a Check-In 40 min	Plan to Use a Check-In 10 min	Try the Habit 3 weeks	Partner Reflection 30 min
PROJECT HABIT: We Kick Off Work **DURATION:** 1 Month	The Great Kick-Off 15 min	Why Kick-Offs Matter 20 min	Role Play Kick-Off 35 min	Plan to Kick Off Work 15 min	Try the Habit 3 weeks	Quadrant Reflection 30 min

You Are Here

You May Have Felt . . . .

 1 Minute  Read on Your Own

As you practiced the Project Habit: We Kick Off Work, it is possible that you felt some of the following emotions:

- Nervousness to kick off work in a new, more defined way
- Satisfaction as you felt the team get clearer on the work's purpose, roles, and roadmap
- Defensiveness as the team asked questions about the work's purpose, roles, and roadmap that you might not yet have answers to
- Energized by the new agility that your team has in adjusting the work plan to meet your project's purpose

On the next page, you'll have an opportunity to reflect on what you tried and how you felt over the past 3 weeks.

DEBRIEF: Reflect on Your Own

 5 Minutes   Write on Your Own

You've tried the Project Habit: We Kick Off Work over the past 3 weeks. Use the quadrant below to reflect on your own. As you reflect on your practice, think about different actions you took and where they fall on the quadrant. This reflection will prepare you to debrief and share as a team.

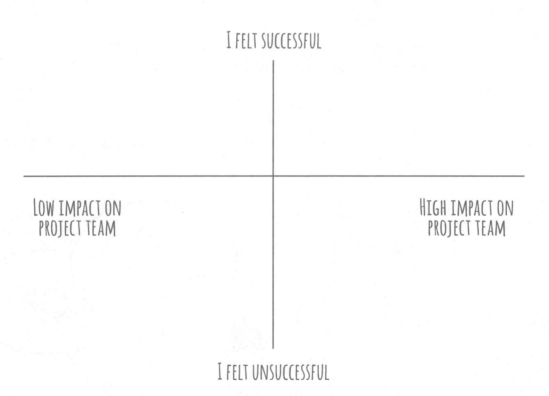

I FELT SUCCESSFUL

LOW IMPACT ON
PROJECT TEAM

HIGH IMPACT ON
PROJECT TEAM

I FELT UNSUCCESSFUL

Share Reflections as a Group

 15 Minutes    Interact as a Team

One of the greatest benefits of building this habit as a team is that you have other people to learn from and share with.

Take 15 minutes to share reflections across the team:

1. Create a chart paper poster of the quadrant.
2. As team members share, have one listener record their sharings on sticky notes and place them on the team quadrant.
3. Once everyone has shared, reflect on any trends you see across the team in terms of actions that were more or less successful and impactful on the project team.

Making the Habit Stick

 2 Minutes    Write on Your Own

This is your third cycle of building a team habit. Revisit your key takeaways from page 72 in Chapter 3 and page 108 in Chapter 4. What is consistent? What new learnings do you have about how you might make this and future habits stick?

Commit to Try the Habit (Again and Again)

 5 Minutes    Interact as a Team

On your own, process the learnings and insights from your team quadrant reflection.
Commit to how you want to continue building the Project Habit: We Kick Off Work.

SHARE THE HABIT!

 AFTERWARD    READ ON YOUR OWN

If you want to share your individual and team learnings about building this project habit, check out the following activities and resources on your own (outside of this team session):

Visit www.newteamhabits.com/project#debrief to access all of these resources.

1. Share your learnings with another team you work with via an e-mail, as part of a newsletter, or in an upcoming conversation or meeting.
2. Connect with others who are practicing this habit on Twitter with #teamhabits.
3. Snap a photo of your reflection page and upload it to our website. Check out other teams' reflections too!

What Comes Next?

 1 Minute　　 Interact as a Team

Congratulations! You've just completed your third and final cycle of The SEPAD Method to build team habits. Here's what to do next:

1. Celebrate! Update your learning plan to record this milestone. Give each other a fun and fancy handshake (we love the Seagull and the Pacman). Check out a student video of 20 fun and fancy handshakes at www.newteamhabits.com/project#debrief.
2. Share with someone outside of this team. Think of yourself as a spark for spreading this habit to other teams.
3. Decide what you want to do next. Chapter 6 has some recommendations.

WE'VE COMPLETED ALL THREE CYCLES OF BUILDING TEAM HABITS FOR LEARNING, MEETINGS, AND PROJECTS!

CHAPTER 6

CONCLUSION

Conclusion

By the time you've completed The SEPAD Method for learning, meetings, and projects, you will feel differently about how you and your team engage in work. You may know your team better. You may have a clearer identity for your team. You may feel like there is more positive energy in your projects.

Just as individuals have habits, good and bad, that shape their personal identity, teams also have habits that shape their group identity. If we want to improve how organizations work, we have to look at how teams function. Think about the organizations you admire, any sports team that is exceptional, or any musical group that creates extraordinary performances. They all have habits and rituals as a team that strengthen their identity through repetition. Little things done often amplify your identity: modeling vulnerability to improve learning, increasing presence through check-ins, and kicking off work to inform purpose and roles. All of these small habits, repeated often, have an amplified effect on the team and organization at large.

Though you've finished working through this guide and practiced three habits, your work is not done. The creation of a lasting habit requires frequent practice and revisiting the five steps of The SEPAD Method to deepen and refine the small habits that lead to a bigger shift in practice.

The SEPAD Method should provide a useful strategy for you and your teams to continue learning and growing.

SPARK: is an objective way to look at a problem of practice so that you aren't stuck in the weeds. It's also a way to ignite inspiration.

EXPAND: should be performed with an open mind to allow for diverse points of view. Discovering new resources should be exciting as you uncover new ideas.

PRACTICE: is required and worth investing the time needed for it if you want to make lasting change and achieve your goals.

APPLY: is about trying small ideas and focusing on achieving small successes over and over again. These successes will provide the confidence and momentum needed to feel like you can push the team a little more.

DEBRIEF: is a way to sort what you want to toss, try again, or retain. The debrief anchors the habits and learnings so that as a team you can evolve through learning together.

We've designed this guide based on hundreds of seminars, workshops, institutes, and conferences, where we had the opportunity to practice over and over in different conditions. Now that you've completed this work with your team, you have a small community to continue learning and practicing with. However, there is also a larger, global community of other practitioners of **The NEW Team Habits** and **The NEW School Rules** books. Reach out to us, tweet your stories, and connect with other leaders to continue learning and sharing. We know learning sticks when you can transfer your knowledge to others.

Learning follows phases, as the Shuhari method of Aikido articulates. First, learn the rule; then, break the rule; finally, be the rule. Only by repeatedly practicing, sharing, refining, and ultimately teaching these responsive habits to others will you master them. So commit to sharing one idea a month with a new person or team. Coach others who are getting started.

Become the expert! Be the rule!

APPENDIX

About the Authors

ANTHONY KIM

Anthony Kim is a nationally recognized leader in education technology, school design, and personalized learning. As founder and CEO of Education Elements, he has been involved in helping hundreds of schools change the way they think about teaching and learning. As the author of "Personalized Learning Playbook: Why the Time Is Now," Anthony has influenced many educators.

He has contributed to many publications on new school models, including "Lessons Learned From Blended Programs: Experiences and Recommendations From the Field." Anthony is a nationally recognized speaker on personalized learning, and his work has been referenced by the Christensen Institute, iNACOL, EdSurge, CompetencyWorks, Education Week, District Administration, and numerous research reports.

Anthony also founded Provost Systems, which provided online learning solutions to school districts. Provost Systems was acquired by EdisonLearning, where Anthony served as executive vice president of online. Anthony is passionate about helping school districts become more nimble, understanding what motivates adult learners, and designing schools that plan for the needs of our future.

Outside of education, Anthony is passionate about triathlons and learning about people who overcome remarkable challenges. He is a San Francisco native and continues to live there with his wife, Angela, and rescued dogs.

Keara Mascareñaz

Keara Mascareñaz is the managing partner, organizational design at Education Elements. She focuses on organizational design and how to build and scale a culture of innovation in large systems. Keara leads work in change management, leadership development, school design, and strategic planning. Keara is the toolkit creator for **The NEW School Rules: 6 Vital Practices for Thriving and Responsive Schools.**

Keara has supported systemwide change at more than 500 district and school partners and has led projects for rural, urban, and suburban schools and districts, including dozens of Gates Foundation Next Generation Learning Challenge schools and regions, Gates Next Generation System Initiative grantees, and Race to the Top district winners. She has been a keynote speaker and workshop facilitator at TinyCon, iNACOL, District Administration Leadership Institute, Blended and Personalized Learning Conference, Personalized Learning Summit, and hundreds of districts around the country.

Keara began her career as a third-grade teacher on the Navajo Reservation. She worked as a college coach, history teacher, operations manager, and curriculum designer. Through this work, she learned how to effectively communicate about and engage folks in the work of large-scale change. Keara was selected as one of twenty fellows in the national Pahara-NextGen network that focuses on developing leaders who will change the future of education. Keara grew up in rural, southern Oregon and currently lives in Denver with her husband.

153

Kawai Lai

Kawai Lai is a designer, facilitator, and strategy consultant helping organizations make the abstract more concrete.

She is also a cofounder of VizLit, an organization with the mission to unlock the visual minds of students and educators.

Formerly, she served as vice president of innovation at the National Association of Independent Schools, a nonprofit serving more than 1,800 schools and 730,000 students across the country and abroad. In her role, she helped schools reimagine education, build capacity to innovate, and share stories of authentic progress.

Kawai was a founding team member of Education Elements, an ed tech startup working with the most forward-thinking public school districts and charters across the country to personalize learning.

Prior to a career in education, Kawai spent a decade in consulting and technology, implementing large-scale technology systems with Deloitte, working in different industries, including health care, biotech, and aerospace.

She has a master of business administration degree from Haas, UC Berkeley, and a bachelor of science in mechanical engineering from Southern Methodist University.

BIBLIOGRAPHY

Babur, Oset. "Talking About Failure Is Crucial for Growth," New York Times, August 17, 2018, https://www.nytimes.com/2018/08/17/smarter-living/talking-about-failure-is-crucial-for-growth-heres-how-to-do-it-right.html

Casali, Davide "Folletto." "Shuhari: A Mental Model for the Phases of Mastery," Intense Minimalism, December 22, 2014, https://intenseminimalism.com/2014/shuhari-a-mental-model-for-the-phases-of-mastery/

CIA Challenge, inspired by Mike Arauz, "The Future of Organizations Is Responsive," https://medium.com/21st-century-organizational-development/the-future-of-organizations-is-responsive-5e2e9b5af16a

Duhigg, Charles. "What Google Learned From the Quest to Build a Perfect Team," New York Times, February 25, 2016, https://www.nytimes.com/2016/02/28/magazine/what-google-learned-from-its-quest-to-build-the-perfect-team.html

Edmondson, Amy. "How Do You Build Psychological Safety?" TEDx Talk, https://www.youtube.com/watch?v=LhoLuui9gX8

Education Elements. "Toolbox: Check In/Check Out," https://www.edelements.com/hubfs/NSR%20Check-in%20Check-out.pdf

Fancy Handshakes, described in Chase Mielke, "19 Twists on the Fist Bump Every Teacher Should Know," We Are Teachers, April 25, 2015, https://www.weareteachers.com/19-twists-on-the-fist-bump-every-teacher-should-know/

Goff-Dupont, Sarah. "Avoid These 5 Mistakes for an Amazing Kick-Off Meeting," Atlassian, June 2018, https://www.atlassian.com/blog/teamwork/kick-off-meeting-agenda-mistakes/amp

Goff-Dupont, Sarah. "Running Effective Meetings: A Guide for Humans," Atlassian, January 1, 2019, https://www.atlassian.com/blog/teamwork/how-to-run-effective-meetings

"How Google Builds the Perfect Team," https://www.youtube.com/watch?v=v2PaZ8NI2T4

Justin, Neal. "Top 10 Reasons We Love David Letterman," Star Tribune, May 5, 2015, http://www.startribune.com/top-10-reasons-we-love-david-letterman/302175441/

"Kicking Off: How to Start a Mission-Driven Team," Parabol Resources, https://www.parabol.co/resources/mission-driven-teamwork/03-kicking-off-a-mission-driven-team

Kim, Anthony, & Gonzales-Black, Alexis. "The NEW School Rules: 6 Vital Practices for Thriving and Responsive Schools" (Thousand Oaks, CA: Corwin, 2018).

LexisClick. "The Importance of a Kick Off Meeting for High Value Partnerships," https://www.lexisclick.com/blog/the-importance-of-a-kick-off-meeting-for-high-value-partnerships

Mr. Whiskers, adapted from Play on Purpose, www.playonpurpose.com

Northrup, Tom. Quote from https://www.goodreads.com/author/show/1617224.Tom_Northup

Project Aristotle. Re:Work, https://rework.withgoogle.com/print/guides/5721312655835136/

Razzetti, Gustavo. "How to Increase Focus at Your Meetings," Liberationist, March 19, 2018, https://blog.liberationist.org/mindset-check-in-how-to-make-your-meetings-more-focused-945ba9911683

Sinek, Simon. "Start With Why: How Great Leaders Inspire Everyone to Take Action" (New York: Portfolio, 2011).

Snowball Sharing, described in Jennifer Gonzalez, "The Big List of Class Discussion Strategies," Cult of Pedagogy, October 15, 2015, https://www.cultofpedagogy.com/speaking-listening-techniques/

"Sprinting: Working in Cycles," Parabol Resources, https://www.parabol.co/resources/mission-driven-teamwork/04-sprinting-working-in-cycles

CORWIN

A SAGE Publishing Company

Helping educators make the greatest impact

CORWIN HAS ONE MISSION: to enhance education through intentional professional learning.

We build long-term relationships with our authors, educators, clients, and associations who partner with us to develop and continuously improve the best evidence-based practices that establish and support lifelong learning.

Leadership That Makes an Impact

**ANTHONY KIM &
ALEXIS GONZALES-BLACK**

Designed to foster flexibility and continuous innovation, this resource expands cutting-edge management and organizational techniques to empower schools with the agility and responsiveness vital to their new environment.

**MICHAEL FULLAN,
JOANNE QUINN, &
JOANNE MCEACHEN**

This book defines what deep learning is and takes up the question of how to mobilize complex whole-system change.

**JOANNE QUINN,
JOANNE MCEACHEN,
MICHAEL FULLAN,
MAG GARDNER, &
MAX DRUMMY**

This resource shows you how to design deep learning, measure progress, and assess the conditions to sustain innovation and mobilization.

ERIC SHENINGER

Lead for efficacy in these disruptive times! Cultivating school culture focused on the achievement of students while anticipating change is imperative.

**JOANNE MCEACHEN
& MATTHEW KANE**

Getting at the heart of what matters for students is key to deeper learning that connects with their lives.

**LEE G. BOLMAN
& TERRENCE E. DEAL**

Sometimes all it takes to solve a problem is to reframe it by listening to wise advice from a trusted mentor.

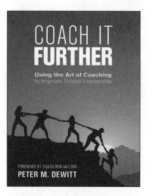

PETER M. DEWITT

This go-to guide is written for coaches, leaders looking to be coached, and leaders interested in coaching burgeoning leaders.

IAN JUKES & RYAN L. SCHAAF

The digital environment has radically changed how students need to learn. Get ready to be challenged to accommodate today's learners.

To order your copies, visit **corwin.com/leadership**

MICHAEL FULLAN

How do you break the cycle of surface-level change to tackle complex challenges? Nuance is the answer.

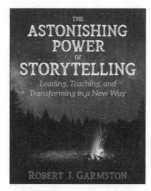

ROBERT J. GARMSTON

Stories have unique power to captivate and motivate action. This guidebook shows how to leverage storytelling to engage students.

JOYCE L. EPSTEIN & ASSOCIATES

Strengthen programs of family and community engagement to promote equity and increase student success!

DEAN T. SPAULDING & GAIL M. SMITH

Help teams navigate the world of data analysis for ongoing school improvement with an easy-to-follow framework that dives deep into data-driven instruction.

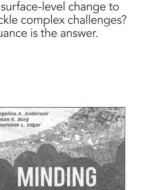

ANGELINE A. ANDERSON, SUSAN K. BORG, & STEPHANIE L. EDGAR

Centered on teacher voice and grounded in foundations of collaboration and data-informed planning, Transform Academy comes to life through its stories and accompanying action steps.

AMY TEPPER & PATRICK FLYNN

Leaders know that feedback is essential to teacher development. This how-to guide helps leaders conduct comprehensive observations, analyze lessons, develop high-leverage action steps, and craft effective feedback.

LYN SHARRATT

Explore 14 essential parameters to guide system and school leaders toward building powerful collaborative learning cultures.

KENNETH LEITHWOOD

By drawing on the numerous cases and stories, educators will gain a deep understanding of how to prepare the next wave of talented school leaders for success.